CIMA

C000090292

MANAGEMENT LEVEL

PAPER P2

ADVANCED MANAGEMENT
ACCOUNTING

AM PRACTICE KIT

FOR EXAMS IN 2018

BPP
LEARNING MEDIA

Fourth edition 2017

ISBNs 9781 5097 1580 0
e ISBN 9781 5097 1592 3

British Library Cataloguing-in-Publication Data
A catalogue record for this book
is available from the British Library

Published by

BPP Learning Media Ltd
BPP House, Aldine Place, 142/144 Uxbridge Road
London W12 8AA

www.bpp.com/learningmedia

Printed in the United Kingdom

Your learning materials, published by BPP Learning
Media Ltd, are printed on paper obtained from
traceable, sustainable sources.

BPP
LEARNING MEDIA

Contents

Question and Answer index

Using your BPP Exam Practice Kit

One of the key criteria for achieving exam success is question practice. There is generally a direct correlation between candidates who study all topics and practise exam questions and those who are successful in their real exams. This Kit gives you ample opportunity for such practice throughout your preparations for your OT exam.

All questions in your exam are compulsory and all the component learning outcomes will be examined so you must **study the whole syllabus**. Selective studying will limit the number of questions you can answer and hence reduce your chances of passing. It is better to go into the exam knowing a reasonable amount about most of the syllabus rather than concentrating on a few topics to the exclusion of the rest.

Practising as many exam-style questions as possible will be the key to passing this exam. You must do questions under **timed conditions**.

Breadth of question coverage

Questions will cover the whole of the syllabus so you must study all the topics in the syllabus.

The weightings in the table below indicate the approximate proportion of study time you should spend on each topic, and is related to the number of questions per syllabus area in the exam.

P2 Advanced Management Accounting Syllabus topics	Weighting
A Cost planning and analysis for competitive advantage	25%
B Control and performance management of responsibility centres	30%
C Long-term decision making	30%
D Management control and risk	15%

The Objective Test exam

The Objective Test exam is a computer based assessment, which is available on demand at assessment centres all year round.

Objective Test exams in each level can be taken in any order, but candidates must pass all the OT exams for a level before they can sit the Integrated Case Study Exam for that level.

Each exam lasts for 90 minutes and the pass mark is 70%.

Results are available shortly after the test has been completed, and the results will include feedback.

The exam will be made up of different types of questions, including:

Question Type	Explanation
Multiple choice	Standard multiple choice items provide four options. One option is correct and the other three are incorrect. Incorrect options will be plausible, so you should expect to have to use detailed, syllabus-specific knowledge to identify the correct answer rather than relying on common sense.
Multiple response	A multiple response item is the same as a multiple choice question, except more than one response is required. You will normally (but not always) be told how many options you need to select.
Drag and drop	Drag and drop questions require you to drag a "token" onto a pre-defined area. These tokens can be images or text. This type of question is effective at testing the order of events, labelling a diagram or linking events to outcomes.
Gap fill	Gap fill (or "fill in the blank") questions require you to type a short numerical response. You should carefully follow the instructions in the question in terms of how to type your answer – eg the correct number of decimal places.
Hot spot	These questions require you to identify an area or location on an image by clicking on it. This is commonly used to identify a specific point on a graph or diagram
Drop-down list	Drop-down lists follow the same principle as multiple choice questions, in that you need to select one option from a pre-defined list. This can be used in conjunction with a gap-fill question: for example, you may be asked to key a numerical answer into a gap-fill box and then select an explanation for the approach you've taken from a drop-down list.

BPP
LEARNING MEDIA

Learning Objectives

The table below has been prepared by CIMA to help you understand the abilities that CIMA is seeking to assess.

Learning objective	Verbs used	Definition	Example question types
1 Knowledge			
What you are expected to know	• List	• Make a list of	MCQ
	• State	• Express, fully or clearly, the details of / facts of	MCQ
	• Define	• Give the exact meaning of	MCQ
2 Comprehension			
What you are expected to understand	• Describe	• Communicate the key features of	Multiple Response
	• Distinguish	• Highlight the differences between	Multiple Response
	• Explain	• Make clear or intelligible / state the meaning or purpose of	Drop down list
	• Identify	• Recognise, establish or select after consideration	Hotspot
	• Illustrate	• Use an example to describe or explain something	Drop down list
3 Application			
How you are expected to apply your knowledge	• Apply	• Put to practical use	Multiple response
	• Calculate/ compute	• Ascertain or reckon mathematically	Number entry
	• Demonstrate	• Prove the certainty or exhibit by practical means	Hotspot
	• Prepare	• Make or get ready for use	Drag and drop
	• Reconcile	• Make or prove consistent / compatible	Drop down list
	• Solve	• Find an answer to	Number entry
	• Tabulate	• Arrange in a table	Drag and drop

Learning objective	Verbs used	Definition	Example question types
4 Analysis			
How you are expected to analyse the detail of what you have learned	• Analyse	• Examine in detail the structure of	Multiple response
	• Categorise	• Place into a defined class or division	Drag and drop
	• Compare and contrast	• Show the similarities and / or differences between	Hotspot
	• Construct	• Build up or complete	Drag and drop
	• Discuss	• Examine in detail by argument	Multiple response
	• Interpret	• Translate into intelligible or familiar terms	Multiple response
	• Prioritise	• Place in order of priority or sequence for action	Drop down list
	• Produce	• Create or bring into existence	Drag and drop
5 Evaluation			
How you are expected to use your learning to evaluate, make decisions or recommendations	• Advise	• Counsel, inform or notify	Multiple response
	• Evaluate	• Appraise or assess the value of	Multiple response
	• Recommend	• Propose a course of action	Multiple response

In your CBA, questions will be set which test up to the cognitive level of the verb in the component learning outcome in each paper's syllabus, so this means they will test up to level five verbs where the learning outcome permits this.

CIMA will limit the number of lower level questions in the exam – so that students will not be able to achieve the pass mark solely based on correctly answering knowledge and comprehension questions. Higher level questions, requiring candidates to demonstrate application, analysis and evaluation skills must be answered correctly for the pass mark to be reached.

Passing the P2 Objective Test exam

Tackling OTQs

- Read, and **re-read the question** to ensure you fully understand what is being asked.

- When starting to read a question, especially one with a lengthy scenario, **read the requirement first**. You will then find yourself considering the requirement as you read the data in the scenario, helping you to focus on exactly what you have to do.

- **Do not spend too much time on one question** - remember you should spend 1½ minutes, on average, per question.

- If you cannot decide between two answers – look carefully and decide whether for one of the options you are making an unnecessary assumption – **do not be afraid of trusting your gut instinct**.

- **Do not keep changing your mind** – research has shown that the first answer that appeals to you is often the correct one.

- Remember that marks are awarded for correct answers, and marks will not be deducted for incorrect answers. Therefore **answer every single question**, even ones you are unsure of.

- Always submit an answer for a given question even if you do not know the answer - **never leave any answers blank**.

- **Pace yourself** - you will need to work through the exam at the right speed. Too fast and your accuracy may suffer, too slow and you may run out of time. Use this Kit to practice your time keeping and approach to answering each question.

- If you are unsure about anything, remember to **ask the test administrator** before the test begins. Once the clock begins ticking, interruptions will not be allowed.

- Remember to **keep moving on!** You may be presented with a question which you simply cannot answer due to difficulty or if the wording is too vague. If you have only approximately 90 seconds per question, and you find yourself spending five minutes determining the answer for a question then your time management skills are poor and you are wasting valuable time.

- If you finish the exam with time to spare, use the rest of the time to **review your answers** and to make sure that you answered every OTQ.

Demonstrating your understanding of P2

You will be expected to display the following qualities:

Business awareness	You are expected to read the business press. This awareness will enable you to apply your knowledge in context when answering questions.
Time management skills	You need to attempt all parts of all questions. So you must work out before you start the exam how much time you will spend on each question. Stick to this!
Flexible thinking	Questions often won't state what technique(s) you should be using. You need to select the appropriate technique yourself.
Evaluation of past and future performance using information provided	You will need to perform calculations that directly evaluate the scenario presented and based on these give advice.
Show strategic awareness	Although this is a Management level paper, the questions will be starting to test your wider awareness of the environment and strategic issues that a company faces. For instance, questions on pricing policy or externally-oriented management accounting techniques will require a strategic view.

All OTQs in all the exams are worth the same number of marks, both in this Kit and in the real exam. However this is an approximate guide: some OTQs are very short and just require a factual selection, which you either know or you don't, while others are more complex, which will inevitably take more time. Note that the real exam will be balanced such that the 'difficulty' of the exam will be fair for all students – the OTQs in this Kit have also been balanced in a similar way.

Using the solutions and feedback

Avoid looking at the answer until you have finished a question. It can be very tempting to do so, but unless you give the question a proper attempt under exam conditions you will not know how you would have coped with it in the real exam scenario.

When you do look at the answer, compare it with your own and give some thought to why your answer was different, if it was.

If you did not reach the correct answer make sure that you work through the explanation or workings provided, to see where you went wrong. If you think that you do not understand the principle involved, work through and revise the point again, to ensure that you will understand it if it occurs in the exam.

Objective test questions

1 Cost analysis and TQM

1.1 **Which THREE of the following statements are true in the context of a just in time (JIT) inventory system?**

☐ It is dependent upon a close and mutually beneficial working relationship with suppliers.
☐ It can result in much reduced inventory holding costs.
☐ It inevitably increases the need for safety inventories.
☐ It requires suppliers to operate sound quality control procedures.
☐ It works best if supplies are obtained from a number of different suppliers.

1.2 RDE plc uses an activity based costing system to attribute overhead costs to its three products. The following budgeted data relates to the year to 31 December 20X8:

Product	X	Y	Z
Production (000 units)	15	25	20
Batch size (000 units)	2.5	5	4

Machine set up costs are caused by the number of batches of each product and have been estimated to be $600,000 for the year.

Calculate the machine set up costs that would be attributed to each unit of product Y.

$ [   ]

1.3 **In a TQM environment, which of the following would be classified as an external failure cost?**

I   Cost of repairing products returned from customers
II   Cost of customer service section
III   Product liability costs
IV   Cost of providing replacement items due to marketing errors

☐ None of the above
☐ All of the above
☐ I only
☐ III only

1.4 **A World Class Manufacturing manufacturer will have a clear manufacturing strategy aimed at which of the following issues?**

I   Customer satisfaction
II   Flexibility
III   Quality and reliability
IV   Overhead recovery

☐ IV only
☐ I only
☐ II and III
☐ I, II and III

1.5 **Which of the following are problems with JIT?**

I   JIT makes the organisation far more vulnerable to disruptions in the supply chain.
II   Wide geographical spread makes JIT difficult.
III   It is not always easy to predict patterns of demand.
IV   There is a risk that stock might become obsolete.

☐   All of them
☐   None of them
☐   I, II and III
☐   I and III

1.6 **Which one of the following statements represents the ultimate aim of Total Quality Management (TQM)?**

☐   Eliminate the costs of poor quality
☐   Eliminate all quality-related costs
☐   Reduce costs of poor quality
☐   Reduce the workforce

1.7 Your company supplies a particular product to customers X and Y. The product has a list price of $40 with a mark-up of 100%.

As Y buys in bulk it receives a discount of 10% for every order of 100 units or more. However, X obtains a discount of 15% whatever the size of the order as it collects the items, thereby saving your company any distribution costs.

The administration cost per order is $40 and distribution costs are $800 per order.

X places 10 orders in the year totalling 400 units, and Y places 5 orders for 100 units each.

Choose which is your most profitable customer.

☐   X
☐   Y

1.8 **In terms of the activity based hierarchy, what type of cost is equipment maintenance?**

☐   Product / process level
☐   Organisational / facility level
☐   Batch level
☐   Unit level

1.9 **The theory of constraints is an approach to production management, which aims to maximise sales revenue less:**

☐   Variable overhead costs
☐   All production costs
☐   Material costs as throughput
☐   Material and variable overhead costs

1.10 **Which two of the following statements do not relate to Kaizen costing?**

☐   Management should investigate and respond when targets are not met.
☐   It assumes continuous improvement.
☐   Targets are set and applied monthly.
☐   It is used for cost control.
☐   Employees are often viewed as the cause of problems.
☐   It is used for cost reduction.

1.11 HDE Co uses activity-based costing to allocate production set-up costs to Products X, Y and Z.

Set-up costs: $95,000

Activity	Product X	Product Y	Product Z
Production runs	50	30	20
Number of inspections	35	45	65
Number of customer orders delivered	20	30	50
Number of purchase orders delivered	30	40	60

Calculate the amount of set-up costs that should be allocated to Product X.

$ [   ]

1.12 JKL Co uses activity-based costing to allocate overheads to products.

Set-up costs:	$40,000
Inspection costs	$37,500
Inventory handling costs:	$13,500

Activity	Product A	Product B	Product C
Production runs	35	40	25
Number of inspections	15	25	35
Number of inventory requisitions	10	15	20

1,000 units of each product will be produced.

Calculate the total overhead per unit of Product A. Answers should be to two decimal places.

$ [   ]

1.13 **Which of the following are included within activity based management (ABM)?**

(a)   Cost reduction
(b)   Product design decisions
(c)   Variance analysis
(d)   Operational control
(e)   Performance evaluation

☐   (a) only
☐   (a), (c), (d) and (e)
☐   (c), (d) and (e) only
☐   (a), (b), (d) and (e) only

1.14 **For which of the following reasons is activity based costing regarded as an improvement on traditional absorption costing?**

I   Recognises the factors which drive costs
II   Addresses all overheads
III   Improves the quality of the costing process

☐   I and III only
☐   I, II and III
☐   II and III only
☐   None of them

1.15 **Which of the following is not a feature of activity based costing?**

I   It recognises that a single factor such as machine hours cannot be the driver of all overhead costs.
II   It seeks to recognise the causes of the costs of activities through the use of cost drivers.
III   It allocates the costs associated with cost drivers into cost pools.
IV   It uses a basis such as labour hours to incorporate overheads into product costs.

☐   None of them
☐   All of them
☐   IV only
☐   II only

1.16 **Which of the following is not considered to be a strength of activity based costing?**

I   Particularly appropriate for an advanced manufacturing technology environment
II   Identifies the driver of the overhead cost
III   Particularly fashionable technique
IV   Recognises the complexity of the production process

☐   All of them
☐   III only
☐   II, III and IV
☐   IV only

1.17 **In activity based costing (ABC), what is a cost driver?**

☐   A mechanism for accumulating the costs of an activity
☐   An overhead cost that is incurred as a direct consequence of an activity
☐   A factor which causes the costs of an activity
☐   A cost relating to more than one product or service

1.18 **Which of the following is an aspect of JIT?**

I   The use of small frequent deliveries against bulk contracts
II   The grouping of machines or workers by product or component instead of by type of work performed
III   A reduction in machine set-up time
IV   Production driven by demand

☐   None of them
☐   All of them
☐   I only
☐   III and IV

1.19 **Which of the following statements about activity based costing is / are correct?**

I   Short-term variable overhead costs should be traced to products using volume-related cost drivers, such as machine hours or direct labour hours.

II Long-term variable production overhead costs are driven partly by the complexity and diversity of production work, as well as by the volume of output.

III Transactions undertaken by support department personnel are the appropriate cost drivers for long-term variable overhead costs.

IV Overheads should be charged to products on the basis of their usage of an activity. A product's usage of an activity is measured by the number of the activity's cost driver it generates.

☐   All of them
☐   I only
☐   II only
☐   I, III and IV

1.20 **An approach of producing goods or purchasing inventory only when required is known as:**

☐   Just-in-time
☐   Ad hoc
☐   Level capacity strategy
☐   Plan-do-check-act (PDCA) quality

1.21 **In Pareto analysis, what is the 80/20 rule?**

I   An approximate rule to the effect that 20% of the products will provide 80% of sales

II An approximate rule to the effect that an increase of 80% in costs will be reflected by a 20% decline in sales

III An approximate rule to the effect that 80% of wealth is held by 20% of the population

IV An approximate rule to the effect that the wealth of the richest 20% of the population equals that of the other 80%

☐   II and III
☐   II only
☐   I only
☐   I and III

---

2 Techniques for enhancing long-term profits

2.1 The following statements have been made about Cam Co's target costing system.

(1) Target costing ensures that new product development costs are recovered in the target price for the webcam.

(2) A cost gap is the difference between the target price and the target cost of the webcam.

Which of the above statements is / are true?

☐   1 only
☐   2 only
☐   Neither 1 nor 2
☐   Both 1 and 2

2.2 Which of these are aspects of value, when applying value analysis?

- ☐ Cost value
- ☐ Exchange value
- ☐ Use value
- ☐ Esteem value
- ☐ Incremental value
- ☐ Target value

2.3 Which one of the following statements is correct?

- ☐ Value engineering is the application of value analysis to existing products.

- ☐ Functional analysis is applied during the maturity stage of a product's lifecycle.

- ☐ Quality function deployment identifies customer requirements and ensures that these drive product design and process planning.

- ☐ Value analysis aims to improve quality even if it increases costs.

2.4 Given the following information, what is the target cost gap for Product P?

Product P target selling price per unit = $20

Target margin on sales = 20%

Current cost = $26

$ ☐☐☐☐☐

2.5 Use the words below to complete the following paragraph.

- • profit
- • logistics
- • support
- • delivery
- • value
- • procurement
- • main
- • primary
- • pressure
- • cost
- • operations

The value chain is the sequence if business activities by which ☐☐☐☐ is added to an organisation's products and services. The ☐☐☐☐ activities include inbound and outbound ☐☐☐☐, marketing and sales and ☐☐☐☐. The ☐☐☐☐ activities include human resource management, firm infrastructure and ☐☐☐☐. A firm is profitable if the value perceived by customers is greater than the ☐☐☐☐ of activities that create that perception.

2.6 Which two of the following methods should be used to move a currently attainable cost closer to target cost?

- ☐ Using standard components wherever possible
- ☐ Acquiring new, more efficient technology
- ☐ Reducing the quality of the product in question
- ☐ Making staff redundant

2.7   A manufacturer of electronic products has designed a new product. The organisation's marketing department believes that 200,000 units of the product could be sold at a price of $25 each. Development and manufacturing costs of the product total $16,000,000. The organisation requires a minimum of 12% return on any investment.

What is an appropriate target cost for the new product?

☐ $25
☐ $9.60
☐ $15.40
☐ $80

2.8   **With what is functional analysis concerned?**

(a)   The functions of a product
(b)   The perceived value of the product to the customer
(c)   The cost of a product

☐   (a) and (c) only
☐   (a) and (b) only
☐   (a) only
☐   (a), (b) and (c)

2.9   **Which of the following are claimed outcomes of value analysis?**

(a)   Elimination of costs
(b)   Reduction of costs
(c)   An increase in sales volumes
(d)   An increase in selling prices

☐   (a) and (b) only
☐   (a), (b) and (c) only
☐   (a), (b), (c) and (d)
☐   (c) and (d) only

2.10   **Use the words below to complete the following paragraph.**

- target
- incremental
- large
- lifecycle
- improve
- kaizen
- fail

A food producer produces one type of low cost food and production techniques have remained largely unchanged for a number of years. It has been struggling with falling sales. The company could improve its position by adopting [＿＿＿] costing. This is applied during the manufacturing stage of the [＿＿＿] and focuses on achieving [＿＿＿] improvements. This type of costing is based on the assumption that the manufacturing process is always able to [＿＿＿].

2.11   **How is target cost calculated?**

☐   Desired selling price minus actual profit margin
☐   Market price minus standard profit margin
☐   Market price minus desired profit margin
☐   Desired selling price minus desired profit margin

2.12 In target costing, what is selling price determined as?

☐ Standard cost plus a profit margin
☐ A competitive market price
☐ Backflush cost plus a profit margin
☐ Total cost plus a profit margin

2.13 The selling price of product B is set at $65 for each item, and sales for the coming year are expected to be 4,000 units.

If the company requires a return of 12% in the coming year on its investment of $900,000 in product B, the target cost for each unit in the coming year is:

☐ $38
☐ $65
☐ $27
☐ $92

2.14 Which two of the following are support activities in the value chain?

☐ Human resource management
☐ Procurement
☐ Service
☐ Operations

2.15 Which of these statements is correct?

i   Target costing aims to reduce costs at the manufacturing stage of a product's lifecycle.
ii   Target costing reflects the critical importance of the development stage of a product's lifecycle.
iii   Kaizen costing is applied during the development stage of a product's lifecycle.
iv   Standard costing emphasises the need for variance analysis for control.

☐ i, ii and iii
☐ i, ii, iii and iv
☐ i and iii
☐ ii and iv

2.16 Which one of the following statements about the value chain is not correct?

☐ The value chain is a model of value and activities and the relationship between them.
☐ Inbound logistics involves the storing of finished goods.
☐ Support activities include infrastructure, technology development, human resources and procurement.
☐ The value chain enables the business to identify potential sources of competitive advantage.

2.17 Which of the following statements about target costing is incorrect?

☐ The first step is to define the product specification.
☐ Required profit is estimated based on profit margins or return on investment.
☐ The cost gap is calculated as the selling price minus the target cost.
☐ Functional analysis is used to close the cost gap before production starts.

2.18 **Given the following information, what is the target cost gap for product X?**

Product X target selling price per unit $10
Target profit   25% on cost
Current cost $8.40 per unit

- ☐ $0.40
- ☐ $0.60
- ☐ $0.90
- ☐ $1.60

2.19 AB plc is a supermarket group which incurs the following costs.

(i)   The bought-in price of the good
(ii)   Inventory financing costs
(iii)   Shelf refilling costs
(iv)   Costs of repacking or 'pack out' prior to storage before sale

AB plc's calculation of direct product profit (DPP) would include:

- ☐   All of the above costs
- ☐   All of the above costs except (ii)
- ☐   All of the above costs except (iv)
- ☐   Cost (i) only

---

3   Cost planning

3.1 T plc has developed a new product, the TF8. The time taken to produce the first unit was 18 minutes.

Assuming that an 80% learning curve applies, the time allowed for the fifth unit (to two decimal places) should be:

Note. For an 80% learning curve $Y = aX^{-0.3219}$

- ☐   5.79 minutes
- ☐   7.53 minutes
- ☐   10.72 minutes
- ☐   11.52 minutes

3.2 **When are the bulk of a product's life cycle costs normally committed?**

- ☐   At the design / development stage
- ☐   When the product is introduced to the market
- ☐   When the product is in its growth stage
- ☐   On disposal

3.3 **Which of the following items would be included in the calculation of the life cycle costs of a product?**

Select all that apply

- ☐   Planning and concept design costs
- ☐   Preliminary and detailed design costs
- ☐   Testing costs
- ☐   Production costs
- ☐   Distribution and customer service costs

3.4 A company is about to commence work on a repeat order for a customer. The item to be manufactured is identical to the first order, and it is expected that a 90% learning curve will apply to the labour operations. The time taken to produce the first item was 100 hours.

If labour is paid at the rate of $7 per hour, the labour cost of manufacturing the second item will be:

☐ $560
☐ $630
☐ $700
☐ $1,260

3.5 **Which three of the following conditions are necessary for learning curve theory to apply?**

☐ A relatively new product
☐ A manual, rather than mechanised production process
☐ A relatively complex production process
☐ Production in batches of equal size
☐ Constant labour wage rates

3.6 A company is considering the price that it should charge for a repeat order. Fifteen units of the product have already been made and supplied to the customer and the company has experienced an 80% learning curve so far. The first unit required 54 hours of labour to complete the manufacture, assembly and testing processes.

Assuming that the 80% learning curve continues, calculate the expected time to be taken for the 16th unit. (to two decimal places)

Note. The learning index for an 80% learning curve is –0.3219.

| | hours

3.7 FH is an electronics company that has developed a new product for the video conferencing market. The product has successfully completed its testing phase and FH has now produced the first four production units. The first unit took three hours of labour time and the total time for the first four units was 8.3667 hours.

Calculate the learning curve improvement rate (rate of learning) to the nearest 0.1%.

| | %

3.8 **In which two circumstances would you not expect learning curve theory to apply?**

☐ When products are made by a highly mechanised process.
☐ When products are brand new.
☐ When products are made largely by labour effort.
☐ When products are made in small quantities for special orders.

3.9 **Life cycle costing is:**

☐ The profiling of cost over a product's production life
☐ The profiling of cost and revenues over a product's production life
☐ The profiling of cost over a product's development, production life and dismantling period
☐ The profiling of cost and revenues over a product's development, production life and dismantling period

3.10 Your company is producing a new product and the costs and sales price associated with the first one produced are:

	$
Materials	6,000
Labour (600 hrs × $6 per hour)	3,600
Overheads (150% of labour costs)	5,400
	15,000
Profit mark-up (20%)	3,000
	18,000

It is planned to sell all products at a 20% mark-up and a 70% learning curve is expected to apply to the production work.

If a customer ordered the first 4 products produced, what would be the average price per product?

$ [   ]

3.11 **In relation to life cycle costing which of the following statements are false?**

☐ Life cycle costing is the profiling of costs over a product's production life.

☐ Life cycle costing aims to minimise cost and maximise sales revenue over the life cycle of the product.

☐ There are five typical stages in the life cycle of a product. These are 'development', 'introduction', 'growth', 'maturity' and 'decline'.

☐ During the 'introduction' stage of the life cycle of a product, the product is likely to be a net user of cash and profits are not expected.

☐ During the 'maturity' stage of the life cycle of a product, the product will be a cash generator and any growth is likely to come from new uses.

3.12 **During which stage of the product life cycle will marketing strategies need to concentrate on differentiating a product from competing products, building brand loyalty and offering incentives to entice competitors' customers to switch?**

☐ Introduction
☐ Growth
☐ Maturity
☐ Decline

3.13 **During the growth stage of the product life cycle, what is the overall aim of the marketing strategies for a product?**

☐ To maintain market share and extend the product's life cycle
☐ To establish a market and build demand
☐ To gain consumer preference and increase sales
☐ To find new uses for the product

3.14 **Which stage of the product life cycle do the following characteristics refer to?**

- New competitors
- Customer feedback received
- New distribution outlets being found
- Product quality improvements made

☐ Introduction
☐ Growth
☐ Maturity
☐ Decline

3.15 A company has developed a new product which it will launch next month. During the initial production phase, the company expects to produce 64 batches of the product. The first batch is expected to require 25 hours of direct labour and the cost of labour is $10 per hour.

A 90% learning curve is expected to apply and the learning index for a 90% learning curve is -0.152.

What is the labour cost of the 64 batches to the nearest $?

$ [   ]

3.16 A company is developing a new product. Production will be in batches of 1,000 units and the direct labour cost is expected to reduce due to the effects of learning for the first 4 batches produced. The direct cost of the first batch of 1,000 units is expected to be $40,000. A 90% learning effect is expected to occur and the learning index for a 90% learning curve is -0.152.

What is the direct labour cost of the 4th batch?

☐ $32,400
☐ $28,056
☐ $129,600
☐ $101,544

3.17 Data relating to the production of the first sixteen batches of a new product are as follows.

Cumulative number of batches	Cumulative total hours
1	1,562.5
16	12,800

The percentage learning effect is closest to:

☐ 45%
☐ 65%
☐ 55%
☐ 85%

3.18 **Which of the following approaches is a cost management tool for reducing the overall cost of a product over its entire life cycle with the help of the production, engineering, research, design, marketing and accounting departments?**

☐ Benchmarking
☐ Kaizen costing
☐ Target costing
☐ Life cycle costing

3.19 When machine time is a binding constraint on production output, which one of the following will have **no effect** on the throughput accounting ratio for a product that the machine is used to manufacture?

☐ Obtaining a lower purchase price for materials for the product
☐ Reducing factory costs
☐ Increasing the selling price of the product
☐ None of the above

4 Pricing

4.1 Market research by Company A has revealed that the maximum demand for product R is 50,000 units each year, and that demand will reduce by 50 units for every $1 that the selling price is increased. Based on this information, Company A has calculated that the profit-maximising level of sales for product R for the coming year is 35,000 units.

At a price of $1,000, no units would be sold.

Calculate the price at which these units will be sold.

$ [   ]

4.2 A company has determined that if a price of $250 is charged for Product G, demand will be 12,000 units. It has also been established that demand will rise or fall by 5 units for every $1 fall/rise in the selling price. The marginal cost of product G is $80.

Marginal revenue $= a - 2bQ$ when the selling price $(P) = a - bQ$,

Calculate the profit-maximising selling price for product G.

$ [   ]

4.3 **Which one of the following statements is true?**

☐ Marginal cost plus pricing is also known as full cost plus pricing.
☐ Minimum pricing is based on relevant costs.
☐ Full cost plus pricing is used for profit maximisation.
☐ Demand is a main factor in the full cost plus approach to pricing.

4.4 **Use the words below to complete the following paragraph.**

- expensive
- decrease
- unique
- late
- skimming
- increase
- early
- penetration

A company manufactures and sells a number of products all of which have a life cycle if six months or less. It has recently developed an innovative product and has decided to launch it with a high price initially as the

product is [   ]. This is a market [   ] pricing strategy which will allow the company to gain

high profits [   ] in the product's lifecycle. In the growth stage, selling prices are likely to

[   ].

4.5 The demand curve for a product is expressed by the formula P = 24 – 0.004Q, where P is the selling price and Q is the quantity demanded per week at that price. At the current sales price of $10 per unit, demand per week is 3,500 units.

By how much could the company raise the selling price per unit in order to increase total sales revenue per week, before total sales revenue per week from the product begins to go into decline?

☐ By $2 per unit
☐ By $4 per unit
☐ By $10 per unit
☐ By $12 per unit

4.6 RJD Ltd makes and sells a single product, Z. The selling price and marginal revenue equations for product Z are as follows:

Selling price = $50 – $0.001x
Marginal revenue = $50 – $0.002x

The variable costs are $20 per unit and the fixed costs are $100,000.

Calculate what the selling price should be in order to maximise profit.

$ [   ]

4.7 A football club charges $12 per ticket for home games. Average attendance at these regular games is 16,000.

When prices were increased by $1 per ticket, attendance fell by 2,500.

Assuming attendance to be purely price dependent, what should be the ticket price to ensure a full house with a capacity of 25,000?

Ticket price should be $ per ticket to the nearest cent.

$ [   ]

4.8 **When is a market penetration pricing policy appropriate?**

☐ If a product is new and different
☐ If demand is highly elastic
☐ If demand is inelastic
☐ If there is no possibility of economies of scale

4.9 **In which one of the following circumstances would the choice of a market skimming pricing policy be unsuitable for a product during the initial stage of its life cycle?**

☐ The product is protected by a patent
☐ Expected demand and the price sensitivity of customers for the new product are unknown
☐ When the product is expected to have a long life cycle
☐ To maximise short-term profitability

4.10 A company has found that for every $15 increase in price, demand for its product would fall by 1,000 units. If the company set the price at $735, only 1,000 units would be demanded.

The costs of producing each unit are as follows:

Direct materials $42
Direct labour $7.90
Fixed overheads $6

What price should be charged for this product to maximise profits?

$ [   ]

4.11 The following information is available for Product Y.

Units	Price	Total revenue	Marginal revenue	Total cost	Marginal cost
	$	$	$	$	$
0	0	0	0	600	–
1	504	504	504	720	120
2	471	942	438	804	84
3	439	1,317	375	864	60
4	407	1,628	311	924	60
5	377	1,885	257	1,005	81
6	346	2,076	191	1,134	129
7	317	2,219	143	1,274	140
8	288	2,304	85	1,440	166
9	259	2,331	27	1,674	234
10	232	2,320	(11)	1,980	306

What is the optimal price for Product Y, if they have to choose from the list of prices in the table above?

$ [   ]

4.12 Product LOO currently sells for $95 per unit. Annual demand at that price is 107,000 units. If the price falls to $85, the annual demand increases by 2,500 units.

What is the formula for the demand curve?

☐ P = 523 – Q/250
☐ P = 523 + Q/250
☐ P = 523 – Q/2,500
☐ P = 137.8 – Q/250

4.13 H is launching a new product. It expects to incur variable costs of $14 per unit.

Market research has been done to determine the optimum selling price with the following results.

If the price charged was to be $25 per unit then the demand would be 1,000 units each period.

For every $1 increase in the selling price, demand would reduce by 100 units each period.

Calculate the optimum selling price for the new product (in cents to two decimal places).

Optimal selling price $ [   ]

4.14 **Which of the following statements best explains the difference between market skimming and penetration pricing?**

☐ Penetration pricing is a strategy that is often used in the decline phase of a product's life cycle whereas market skimming is a strategy that is mainly used in the introduction phase of the product life cycle.

☐ Market skimming is a strategy that is often used in the decline phase of a product's life cycle whereas penetration pricing is a strategy that is mainly used in the introduction phase of the product life cycle.

☐ Penetration pricing is a policy of charging high prices when the product is first launched in order to obtain sufficient penetration in the market whereas market skimming is a policy of charging low prices when a product is first launched and attracting customers through heavy advertising and sales promotion.

☐ A strategy of penetration pricing could be effective in discouraging potential new entrants to the market whereas the strategy of market skimming is to gain high unit profits early in the products life cycle.

4.15 An entertainment company is launching a new games console to the market next year and is currently considering its pricing strategy for this new product.

The product will be unlike any other product that is currently available and will introduce 3D effects when playing games online. The prototype required a substantial amount of time to develop and as a result the company is keen to recover its considerable research and development costs as soon as possible.

However, this unique position in the market place is expected to remain for only six months before one of the company's competitors develops a similar games console. The competitors would avoid the significant research and development costs by reverse engineering this company's own product.

To minimise the effect of this, this company must be prepared to reduce the price of the product significantly just before its competitors enter the market.

Which pricing strategy would be most suitable during the launch phase of the games console?

☐ Penetration pricing
☐ Market skimming
☐ Dual pricing
☐ 'Own label' pricing

4.16 **Which of these statements are correct?**

i It is worthwhile for a company to sell further units when the marginal revenue is greater than the marginal cost

ii Price is the only factor affecting demand

iii Premium pricing is used to imply that the product is different in some way

iv Loss leadership is often used for new and different products with a short product lifecycle

☐ (i), (ii), (iii)
☐ (i), (ii), (iii), (iv)
☐ (i), (iii)
☐ (ii), (iv)

4.17 A company has recently developed an innovative product. Since the product is unique, it was decided that it would be launched with a market skimming pricing policy. However, the company expects that other companies will try to enter the market very soon.

Which of the following statements is likely to be incorrect?

☐ In the growth stage, the selling price is likely to fall as competition increases.
☐ In the growth stage, costs are likely to be increasing.
☐ At the maturity stage, the selling price will probably have stabilised.
☐ The company needs to make as much profit as possible in the early part of the lifecycle.

4.18 A company is selling a product for $180. At this price it sells 50,000 units per month. The variable cost of sale per unit is $125 and monthly fixed costs are $2 million. It has been estimated that for every $10 increase or reduction in price, sales demand will fall or increase by 4,000 units.

At what selling price per unit will the monthly profit be maximised?

☐ $135
☐ $180
☐ $215
☐ $248.75

4.19 Market research into demand for a product indicates that when the selling price per unit is $145, demand in each period will be 5,000 units and if the price is $120, demand will be 11,250 units. It is assumed that the demand function for this product is linear. The variable cost per unit is $27.

What selling price should be charged in order to maximise the monthly profit?

☐ $83
☐ $84
☐ $95
☐ $96

4.20 **For which one of the following reasons would the choice of penetration pricing be unsuitable for a product during the initial stage of its life cycle?**

☐ To discourage new entrants to the market
☐ To increase the length of the initial stage of the life cycle
☐ To achieve economies of scale
☐ To set a price for a product that has a high price elasticity of demand

5 Decision making in responsibility centres

5.1 **A flexible budget is a budget that:**

☐ Is changed during the budget period according to changed circumstances

☐ Is continuously updated by adding a further accounting period when the earliest accounting period has expired

☐ Results from the participation of budget holders

☐ Recognises different cost behaviour patterns and is designed to change as the volume of activity changes

5.2 **Which of the following statements are true?**

    I   A flexible budget can be used to control operational efficiency.

    II   Incremental budgeting can be defined as a system of budgetary planning and control that measures the additional costs that are incurred when there are unplanned extra units of activity.

    III   Rolling budgets review and, if necessary, revise the budget for the next quarter to ensure that budgets remain relevant for the remainder of the accounting period.

    ☐   I and II only
    ☐   II and III only
    ☐   III only
    ☐   I only

5.3 The board of directors of X plc has agreed a budget that reflects significant savings brought about by new working practices. However, at the recommendation of the Finance Director, a contingency has been included in the budget to allow for the fact that not all improvements will come to fruition in reality.

What type of standard has been used to set this budget?

    ☐   Ideal
    ☐   Attainable
    ☐   Current
    ☐   Basic

5.4 The following information is available regarding the fixed budget of HU Co.

Production units sold	5,000
Budget	$'000
Sales	35
Variable costs	20
Contribution	15
Fixed costs	10
Profit	5

Calculate the profit figure if the number of production units sold is flexed to 8,000.

Ignore any movements in inventory.

$ [＿＿＿＿＿] ,000

5.5 **Which of the following weaknesses in a budgeting system is most likely to be found in a top-down system of budgeting?**

    ☐   Budgets may include excessive amounts of 'slack' (unnecessary budget spending allowances).
    ☐   Budgets may be inconsistent with the long-term strategy of the organisation.
    ☐   Budgets may not be realistic in practice.
    ☐   Budgets may lack credibility with senior management.

5.6 **Which of the following statements is / are correct?**

    (i)   Fixed budgets are not useful for control purposes.
    (ii)   A prerequisite of flexible budgeting is a knowledge of cost behaviour patterns.
    (iii)   Budgetary control procedures are useful only to maintain control over an organisation's expenditure.

    ☐   (i), (ii) and (iii)
    ☐   (i) and (ii) only
    ☐   (ii) and (iii) only
    ☐   (ii) only

5.7 Extracts from the flexible budgets of a manufacturing company are as follows.

Production and sales quantity	5,000 units	7,000 units
Budget cost allowance	$'000	$'000
Materials costs	50	70
Labour costs	65	77
Production overheads	80	84
Administration costs	35	35
Selling and distribution costs	15	19
Total cost allowance	245	285

What would be the expected total expenditure incurred in a period when 6,000 units are produced and 5,500 units are sold?

$ _____

5.8 **Budgeting has been criticised extensively by the Beyond Budgeting Round Table (BBRT). Which of the following is NOT a criticism of traditional budgeting by the BBRT?**

☐ Budgets protect rather than reduce costs.

☐ Budgets focus on sales targets rather than customer satisfaction.

☐ Managers do not give budgeting enough of their time.

☐ Budgets discourage innovation and initiative.

5.9 **Which two of the following are fundamental concepts that underlie the Beyond Budgeting® approach?**

☐ Use adaptive management processes rather than the more rigid annual budget

☐ Use traditional budgeting in conjunction with other techniques

☐ Move towards centralised hierarchies rather than devolved networks

☐ Move towards devolved networks rather than centralised hierarchies

---

5.10 The following statements have been made about planning and operational variances.

(1) They can undermine the importance placed on the original targets set at the beginning of the budgeting period.

(2) It is usually easy to identify in retrospect what prices and quantities were, but not nearly so easy to identify what they should have been.

Which of the above statements is / are true?

☐ 1 only

☐ 2 only

☐ Neither 1 nor 2

☐ Both 1 and 2

5.11 A manager of a production department in a manufacturing company is made responsible for certain costs of his department.

Which of the following costs should the manager not be held accountable for?

☐ A proportion of rent and rates for the building the production department shares with other departments

☐ Direct labour costs

☐ Direct material costs

☐ Repair costs incurred on machinery in the production department arising from misuse by production department employees

5.12 **Which of the following is not an advantage of a participative budget?**

☐ Morale and motivation is improved.
☐ Specific resource requirements are included.
☐ They do not take much time to prepare.
☐ Knowledge is shared between different levels of management.

5.13 **In adaptive processes, described in the Beyond Budgeting® model, goals should be based on:**

☐ Maximising profit
☐ Maximising return on investment
☐ Maximising performance potentials
☐ Maximising available cash

5.14 **Which two of the following are adverse consequences of a 'bottom up' approach to budgeting?**

☐ In general they are unrealistic.
☐ Managers may introduce budgetary slack.
☐ Managers may set easy budgets to ensure they are achievable.
☐ Specific resource requirements may be overlooked.

5.15 Hay budgeted to sell 400 units and produced the following budget.

	$
Sales	142,000
Variable labour costs	(63,200)
Variable material costs	(25,200)
Contribution	53,600
Fixed costs	(37,800)
Profit	15,800

Actual sales were 460 units which sold for a total of $150,000. Actual expenditure on material was $48,000, actual labour cost was $54,000 and fixed costs totalled $20,000.

What contribution (in $) will a budget that has been flexed to reflect actual output show?

$ ▢

5.16 A divisional manager has developed a budget and just submitted it to a superior.

Which of the following could be used to describe this budget?

☐ Participative
☐ Top down
☐ Imposed
☐ Negotiated

5.17 **Which of the following statements about setting budget targets is / are correct?**

(1) Setting 'ideal standards' as targets for achievement should motivate employees to perform to the best of their ability.

(2) Setting low standards as targets for achievement should motivate employees because they should usually achieve or exceed the target.

☐ 1 only is correct
☐ 2 only is correct
☐ Neither 1 nor 2 is correct
☐ Both 1 and 2 are correct

5.18   **The term 'budget slack' refers to the:**

    ☐   Lead time between the preparation of the master budget and the commencement of the budget period

    ☐   Difference between the budgeted output and the actual output achieved

    ☐   Additional capacity available which is budgeted for even though it may not be used

    ☐   Deliberate overestimation of costs and / or underestimation of revenues in a budget

5.19   **Which one of the following is not usually a consequence of divisionalisation?**

    ☐   Duplication of some activities and costs

    ☐   Goal congruence in decision making

    ☐   Faster decision making at operational level

    ☐   Reduction in head office control over operations

6   Performance measurement

6.1   **Which of the following types of benchmarking involves reviewing the processes of a business to identify those which indicate a problem and offer a potential for improvement?**

    ☐   Competitive

    ☐   Metric

    ☐   Diagnostic

    ☐   Process

6.2   Division B of BM Ltd is considering a project which will increase annual net profit after tax by $15,000, but will require average stock levels to increase by $100,000. The current target return on investment is 10% and the imputed interest cost of capital is 9%.

    In these circumstances would the return on investment (ROI) and / or residual income (RI) criteria motivate the managers of division B to act in the interests of the group as a whole?

    ☐   ROI – yes, RI – yes

    ☐   ROI – yes, RI – no

    ☐   ROI – no, RI – yes

    ☐   ROI – no, RI – no

6.3   A division with $21m capital employed currently earns a return on investment of 16% per annum which is double its cost of capital. It has the opportunity to invest $4m in a new project where the return will be $0.8m per annum over the 4 years of the project. After the fourth year there will be no further returns.

    What would be the division's residual income for the first year if the project is accepted (ignore depreciation)?

    $ ☐ m

6.4   **Which of the following statements about EVA® is / are correct:**

    (i)   EVA® is equal to the net operating profit after tax (NOPAT) less a capital charge, where the capital charge is the weighted average cost of capital multiplied by net assets.

    (ii)   EVA® is based on economic profit which is derived by making a series of adjustments to accounting profits.

    (iii) EVA® is an absolute measure, as compared to a relative one such as ROCE.

    ☐   (i), (ii) and (iii)

    ☐   (i) and (ii) only

    ☐   (ii) and (iii) only

    ☐   (ii) only

6.5　**Which one of the following is not one of the four perspectives of Kaplan and Norton's balanced scorecard?**

☐　Financial perspective
☐　Customer perspective
☐　Internal business perspective
☐　Environmental perspective

6.6　Summary financial statements are given below for one division of a large divisionalised company.

Summary Divisional Financial Statements for the year to 31 December

Balance sheet	$'000	Income statement	$'000
Non-current assets	1,500	Revenue	4,000
Current assets	600	Operating costs	3,600
Total assets	2,100	Operating profit	400
		Interest paid	70
Divisional equity	1,000	Profit before tax	330
Long-term borrowings	700		
Current liabilities	400		
Total equity and liabilities	2,100		

The cost of capital for the division is estimated at 12% each year.

Annual rate of interest on the long term loans is 10%.

All decisions concerning the division's capital structure are taken by central management.

The divisional return on investment (ROI) for the year ended 31 December is:

☐　19.0%
☐　19.4%
☐　23.5%
☐　33.0%

6.7　Summary financial statements are given below for one division of a large divisionalised company.

Summary Divisional Financial Statements for the year to 31 December

Balance sheet	$	Income statement	$
Non-current assets	1,500	Revenue	4,000
Current assets	600	Operating costs	3,600
Total assets	2,100	Operating profit	400
		Interest paid	70
Divisional equity	1,000	Profit before tax	330
Long-term borrowings	700		
Current liabilities	400		
Total equity and liabilities	2,100		

The cost of capital for the division is estimated at 12% each year.

Annual rate of interest on the long term loans is 10%.

All decisions concerning the division's capital structure are taken by central management.

The divisional residual income (RI) for the year ended 31 December is:

☐　$160,000
☐　$196,000
☐　$230,000
☐　$330,000

6.8 Division A of G Ltd reported net profit of $1,700,000 in 20X5 and the gross capital employed at the end of the year was $5,000,000. For evaluation purposes, all divisional assets are valued at original cost. The division is considering a project which will increase annual net profit by $75,000, but will require average inventory levels to increase by $150,000 and non-current assets to increase by $350,000. G Ltd imposes a 18% capital charge on its divisions.

In these circumstances, will the return on investment (ROI) and / or residual income (RI) criteria motivate the managers of division A to accept the project?

☐ ROI – yes, RI – yes
☐ ROI – yes, RI – no
☐ Impossible to tell from the information provided
☐ ROI – no, RI – yes
☐ ROI – no, RI – no

6.9 Division Y has reported annual operating profits of $40.2 million. This was after charging $6 million for the full cost of launching a new product that is expected to last 3 years. Division Y has a risk adjusted cost of capital of 11%. The historical cost of the assets in Division Y, as shown on its balance sheet, is $100 million, and the replacement cost has been estimated at $172 million.

Ignore the effects of taxation.

The EVA for Division Y is:

☐ $23.28 million
☐ $24.84 million
☐ $29.20 million
☐ $30.44 million

6.10 The following data have been extracted from a company's year-end accounts:

	$
Turnover	7,055,016
Gross profit	4,938,511
Operating profit	3,629,156
Non-current assets	4,582,000
Cash at bank	4,619,582
Short term borrowings	949,339
Trade receivables	442,443
Trade payables	464,692

Calculate the return on capital employed to the nearest whole %.

☐

6.11 **The time taken for a company to develop new products would be included in which perspective of the balanced scorecard?**

☐ Financial
☐ Customer
☐ Internal
☐ Innovation and learning

6.12 A division of a service company is aware that its recent poor performance has been attributable to a low standard of efficiency amongst the workforce, compared to rival firms. The company is adopting a balanced scorecard approach to setting performance targets. As part of its objective of closing the skills gap between itself and rival companies, the division's management has set a target of providing at least 40 hours of training each year for all its employees.

This is a performance target that reflects:

- ☐ A finance perspective
- ☐ An internal process perspective
- ☐ A learning and growth perspective
- ☐ A customer perspective

6.13 **In the context of a balanced scorecard approach to the provision of management information, which of the following measures would be appropriate for monitoring the customer perspective?**

(i) Percentage of on-time deliveries
(ii) Customer complaints per month
(iii) Average set-up time

- ☐ (i) and (ii) only
- ☐ (i) and (iii) only
- ☐ (ii) and (iii) only
- ☐ (i), (ii) and (iii)

6.14 **Please complete the following sentence using one of the options below.**

Asset turnover is a measure of:

- ☐ How often on average business assets are replaced
- ☐ How well the assets of a business are used to generate sales
- ☐ How well the assets of a business are used to generate profits
- ☐ The proportion of revenue that is re-invested in assets

6.15 **Which of the following is a non-financial performance measure?**

- ☐ Share price
- ☐ Delivery time
- ☐ Cash flow
- ☐ Revenue

6.16 A company reports sales of $550,000 and a PBIT of $27,500. Its ROCE is 15%.

What is the asset turnover for the company?

☐

6.17 **Which type of benchmarking would be most likely to use reverse engineering?**

- ☐ Internal
- ☐ Functional
- ☐ Competitive
- ☐ Strategic

6.18 The annual operating statement for a company is shown below:

	$'000
Sales revenue	800
Less variable costs	390
Contribution	410
Less fixed costs	90
Less depreciation	20
Net income	300
Assets	$6.75m

The cost of capital is 13% per annum.

The residual income (RI) for the company is closest to:

☐   -$467,000
☐   -$487,000
☐   -$557,000
☐   -$577,500

6.19 The annual operating statement for a company is shown below:

	$'000
Sales revenue	800
Less variable costs	390
Contribution	410
Less fixed costs	90
Less depreciation	20
Net income	300
Assets	$6.75m

The return on investment (ROI) for the company is closest to:

☐   4.44%
☐   4.74%
☐   5.77%
☐   6.07%

6.20 A company has a call centre to handle queries and complaints from customers. The company is concerned about the average length of calls and the time that it takes to deal with customers. As part of its balanced scorecard, it has set a target for reducing the average time per customer call.

A target for reducing the average time per call would relate to which one of the four balanced scorecard perspectives?

☐   Customer perspective
☐   Financial perspective
☐   Innovation and learning perspective
☐   Internal business (operational) perspective

7 Transfer pricing

7.1 The following statements have been made about a transfer pricing system where Division A transfers output to Division B.

(1) Internal transfers should usually be preferred when there is an external market for the transferred item, because there will be more control over quality and delivery.

(2) The transfer price will determine how profits will be shared between the two divisions.

Which of the above statements is / are true?

☐ 1 only
☐ 2 only
☐ Neither 1 nor 2
☐ Both 1 and 2

7.2 WX has two divisions, Y and Z. The following budgeted information is available.

Division Y manufactures motors and budgets to transfer 60,000 motors to Division Z and to sell 40,000 motors to external customers.

Division Z assembles food mixers and uses one motor for each food mixer produced.

The standard cost information per motor for Division Y is as follows:

	$
Direct materials	70
Direct labour	20
Variable production overhead	10
Fixed production overhead	40
Fixed selling and administration overhead	10
Total standard cost	150

In order to set the external selling price the company uses a 33.33% mark-up on total standard cost.

Calculate the budgeted profit / (loss) for Division Y if the transfer price is set at marginal cost.

$ ☐

Calculate the budgeted profit / (loss) for Division Y if the transfer price is set at the total production cost.

$ ☐

7.3 **Which two of the following are reasons why cost-based approaches to transfer pricing are often used in practice?**

☐ Because there is often no external market for the product that is being transferred
☐ Because the external market is imperfect
☐ Because the transferring division wants to maximise its profits
☐ Because the buying division wants to maximise its profits

7.4 ABC Group has several divisions. Division A manufactures one type of product, a Unit, which it sells both to external customers and also to Division B, another member of the ABC Group. The Group's policy is to allow divisions the freedom to set transfer prices and choose their own suppliers.

ABC uses residual income (RI) to assess divisional performance with targets being set each year. The group's cost of capital is 10% a year. For Division A the budgeted information for next year is as follows:

Maximum capacity	200,000 units
External sales	160,000 units
External selling price	$33 per unit
Variable cost	$20 per unit
Fixed costs	$1,200,000
Capital employed	$3,600,000
Target RI	$200,000

Division B provisionally requests a quote for 60,000 Units from Division A for the coming year.

What is the transfer price per Unit that Division A should quote B in order to meet its residual income target?

$ ☐ per unit.

7.5 ABC Group has several divisions. Division A manufactures one type of product, a Unit, which it sells both to external customers and also the Division B, another member of the ABC Group. The Group's policy is to allow divisions the freedom to set transfer prices and choose their own suppliers.

ABC uses residual income (RI) to assess divisional performance with targets being set each year. The group's cost of capital is 10% a year.

For Division A the budgeted information for next year is as follows:

Maximum capacity	200,000 units
External sales	160,000 units
External selling price	$33 per unit
Variable cost	$20 per unit
Fixed costs	$1,200,000
Capital employed	$3,600,000
Target RI	$200,000

Division B provisionally requests a quote for 60,000 Units from Division A for the coming year.

What transfer price(s) would Division A have to quote Division B if the Group's policy is to quote transfer prices based on opportunity costs?

☐ $33 only
☐ $33 and $20
☐ $20 only
☐ None of these

7.6 Jim Jarr plc is a manufacturing company with several divisions. Division X produces a single product which it sells to Division Y and also to outsiders.

	Sales to Div Y by Div X $	External sales by Div X $
Sales revenue: at $35 per unit		350,000
at $30 per unit	150,000	
Variable costs at $18 per unit	(90,000)	(180,000)
Contribution	60,000	170,000
Fixed costs	(50,000)	(120,000)
Profit	10,000	50,000

A supplier offers to supply 4,000 units at $25 each to Division Y.

What will Division X's contribution be if Division X does not match the lower price offered by the external supplier and cannot increase its external sales, so that Division Y chooses to purchase from the external supplier?

$ _____

7.7 A company has three profit centres, X, Y and Z. The output of division X is transferred to division Y, and the output of division Y is transferred to division Z. The end product of Z is sold to external customers, at a price of $100 per unit. The transfer prices of output transferred between profit centres, are based on a profit margin of 20%.

Cost data is as follows, excluding transfer costs.

	X $ per unit	Y $ per unit	Z $ per unit
Added materials	8	6	6
Direct labour	6	4	8
Production overhead	10	10	12

What is the profit per unit sold for profit centre Z?

(in dollars and cents)

$ _____

7.8 X and Y are two divisions of Oldhat Ltd. Division X manufactures one product, the XX, with a unit production cost of $12 which includes $2 of absorbed fixed overhead. The prevailing market price for the XX is $16. Product XX is sold outside the company in a perfectly competitive market and also to division Y. If sold outside the company, variable selling costs of $2 per unit are incurred.

If the total demand for the XX is more than sufficient for division X to manufacture to capacity, what would be the minimum price division X would accept to transfer the XX to division Y?

☐ $10
☐ $12
☐ $14
☐ $16

7.9 If transfer prices are set at variable cost, the supplying division does not cover its fixed costs.

Which of the following does not resolve this problem?

☐ Each division can be given a share of the overall contribution earned by the organisation.
☐ Central management can impose a range within which the transfer price should fall.
☐ A two-part charging system can be adopted.
☐ A system of dual pricing can be adopted.
☐ The level of fixed costs can be reduced.

7.10 Within the PQ Group plc, division P transfers component X to division Q at a transfer price of $52 per unit. The unit cost of X within division P is $45 (variable cost of $34 plus absorbed fixed overhead of $11). Division Q has located an external supply of component X for $49 per unit.

If division Q uses the external supplier, what will be the effect on profits?

☐ P's profit will decrease, overall group profit will decrease
☐ P's profit will increase, overall group profit will decrease
☐ P's profit will decrease, overall group profit will increase
☐ P's profit will increase, overall group profit will increase
☐ It is not possible to tell without further information

7.11 ABC Group has several divisions. Division A manufactures one type of product, a Unit, which it sells both to external customers and also the Division B, another member of the ABC Group. The Group's policy is to allow divisions the freedom to set transfer prices and choose their own suppliers.

ABC uses residual income (RI) to assess divisional performance with targets being set each year. The group's cost of capital is 12% a year. For Division A the budgeted information for next year is as follows:

Maximum capacity	200,000 units
External sales	160,000 units
External selling price	$33 per unit
Variable cost	$20 per unit
Fixed costs	$1,200,000
Capital employed	$3,600,000
Target RI	$200,000

Division A needs to meet its target RI and sets its transfer price at $20.20 accordingly. Division B, based in a different country to A, needs 60,000 Units which it could purchase from Division A, but it could also buy them from W Co at $20 per Unit. Division A is taxed at 50%, whilst Division B is taxed at 30%.

By how much would the group's profits increase if B bought from W rather than A?

$ ☐

7.12 Which of the following is not one of the desired effects of an 'ideal' transfer price?

☐ It enables the transferring division to earn a return for its efforts.
☐ It enables profit centre performance to be measured commercially.
☐ It enables profit centres to make entirely autonomous decisions.
☐ It results in action that is consistent with the aims of the organisation as a whole.

7.13 **In which two of the following situations should market price or market based price be used as a basis for transfer pricing?**

☐ When variable costs and market prices are constant
☐ When there is an imperfect external market
☐ When variable costs and market prices are not constant
☐ When a perfect external market exists

7.14 **The following sentence can be validly completed by selecting which two options from below?**

When there is no external market for an item being transferred between divisions the transfer price should be:

☐ Less than or equal to the selling price minus variable costs in the receiving division
☐ Greater than or equal to the selling price minus variable costs in the receiving division
☐ Less than or equal to the variable cost in the supplying division
☐ Greater than or equal to the variable cost in the supplying division

7.15 Consider two profit centres, M and S. M transfers all its output to S as there is no external market for it. The variable cost of output from M is $4 a unit, and fixed costs are $1,000 per month.

Additional processing costs in S are $5 a unit for variable costs, plus fixed costs of $950 per month. Budgeted production is 500 units a month, and the output of S sells for $14 a unit.

Which of the following transfer prices will motivate the managers of both M and S to increase output?

☐ $6.00
☐ $4.00
☐ $9.50
☐ $14.00

7.16 **Which TWO of the following are reasons to use market value as a transfer price?**

☐ The market price is subject to wide fluctuations
☐ As an incentive to control costs
☐ There is no external market for the product being transferred
☐ The supplying division is being assessed as a profit centre

7.17 **Which of the following is not a feature of a two-part tariff system?**

☐ Once a period there is a transfer of a fixed fee as a lump sum payment to the supplying division.
☐ Transfer prices are set at variable cost.
☐ The selling division's fixed costs should be covered.
☐ The message sent to the supplying division is that fixed costs must be controlled.

7.18 **Which of the following is not a consideration exclusive to multinational companies when establishing transfer prices?**

☐ Taxation
☐ Goal congruence
☐ Tariffs
☐ Anti-dumping legislation

8 Project appraisal

8.1 A project has a cash outflow of $7,000 at time 0 and cash inflows of $5,000 at time 1, $800 at time 2 and $2,700 at time 3.

If the cost of capital is 15% per annum, calculate the net present value of the project. (to two decimal places)

$ [   ]

8.2 **Indicate whether, in a comparison of the NPV and IRR techniques, the following statements are true or false.**

(a) Both methods give the same accept or reject decision, regardless of the pattern of the cash flows

☐ True ☐ False

(b) IRR is technically superior to NPV and easier to calculate

☐ True ☐ False

(c) The NPV approach is superior if discount rates are expected to vary over the life of the project

☐ True ☐ False

(d) NPV and accounting ROCE can be confused

☐ True ☐ False

8.3 A project has a NPV of $49m at a discount rate of 10% and a NPV of $18m at a discount rate of 15%.

Calculate the internal rate of return on the project to the nearest 0.1%.

[   ] %

8.4 A company has determined that the net present value of an investment project is $12,304 when using a 10% discount rate and $(3,216) when using a discount rate of 15%.

Calculate the internal rate of return on the project to the nearest 1%.

[   ] %

8.5 A company has a nominal (money) cost of capital of 18% per annum.

If inflation is 6% each year, calculate the company's real cost of capital to the nearest 0.01%.

[   ] %

8.6 **What are the disadvantages of the payback method of investment appraisal?**

I   It tends to maximise financial and business risk.
II   It is a fairly complex technique and not easy to understand.
III It cannot be used when there is a capital rationing situation.

☐ None of the above
☐ All of the above
☐ I only
☐ II and III

8.7 Tree Cole Tarts plc is appraising an investment of $700,000 in plant, which will last four years and have no residual value. Fixed operating costs (excluding depreciation) will be $200,000 in the first year, increasing by 5% per annum because of inflation. The contribution in the first year is forecast at $620,000, increasing by 7% per annum due to inflation. The company's money cost of capital is 14%.

Calculate the net present value of the investment, to the nearest $'000.

$ [   ]

8.8 M plc is evaluating three possible investment projects and uses a 10% discount rate to determine their net present values.

Investment		A	B	C
		$'000	$'000	$'000
Initial Investment		400	450	350
Incremental cash flows:	Year 1	100	130	50
	Year 2	120	130	110
	Year 3	140	130	130
	Year 4	120	130	150
	Year 5	100	150	100
Net present value		39	55	48

Calculate the discounted payback period of investment B. (to 1 decimal place)

[   ] years

8.9 A company is considering an investment of $400,000 in new machinery. The machinery is expected to yield incremental profits over the next five years as follows:

Year	Profit
	($)
1	175,000
2	225,000
3	340,000
4	165,000
5	125,000

Thereafter, no incremental profits are expected and the machinery will be sold. It is company policy to depreciate machinery on a straight line basis over the life of the asset. The machinery is expected to have a value of $50,000 at the end of year 5.

Calculate the payback period of the investment in this machinery to the nearest 0.1 years.

[   ] years

8.10 An investment has a net present value of $35,000 at 2% and $15,000 at 8%.

What is the approximate internal rate of return?

☐ 10.5%
☐ 12.5%
☐ 9.5%
☐ 8%

8.11 A lease agreement has a net present value of $26,496 at a rate of 8%. The lease involves an immediate down payment of $10,000 followed by 4 equal annual payments.

What is the amount of the annual payment, to the nearest $?

$ [   ]

8.12 Peter plans to buy a holiday villa in five years' time for cash. He estimates the cost will be $1.5m. He plans to set aside the same amount of funds at the beginning of each of the next 5 years, starting immediately and earning a rate of 10% interest per annum compound.

To the nearest $100, how much does he need to set aside each year?

$ [   ]

8.13 Mesma Co pays corporation tax at a rate of 30%. Writing down allowances (WDAs) are given on a 25% reducing balance.

In 20X0 Mesma Co purchases plant and equipment of $100,000 and claims a writing down allowance in that year.

How much tax will Mesma Co save in 20X1 by taking the writing down allowance?

$ [   ]

8.14 **Which ONE of the following statements concerning the modified internal rate of return (MIRR) is correct?**

- ☐ MIRR is based on the cost of capital set by the central bank.
- ☐ MIRR does not discount future cash flows.
- ☐ MIRR is calculated on the basis of investing the inflows at the cost of capital.
- ☐ MIRR is only concerned with capital inflows.

8.15 The following information is available concerning a proposed investment by Emand Co. The company's cost of capital is 10%.

Year	Cash flow
	$
0	(24,500)
1	15,000
2	15,000
3	3,000
4	(3,000)

Calculate the modified internal rate of return (MIRR), to the nearest %

[   ] %

8.16 **The payback period is the number of years that it takes a business to recover its original investment from net returns calculated on what basis?**

- ☐ Before depreciation and before taxation
- ☐ Before depreciation but after taxation
- ☐ After depreciation but before taxation
- ☐ After depreciation and after taxation

8.17 **To what does the internal rate of return equate the present value of expected future net cash receipts?**

☐ Initial cost of the investment outlay
☐ Depreciated value of the investment
☐ Terminal (compound) value of future cash receipts
☐ Zero

8.18 A company is considering whether to invest in a project that would involve the purchase of equipment costing $300,000. The project would have a six-year life, at the end of which the equipment would have an expected residual value of $60,000. Depreciation would be charged using the straight-line method, over the six-year period. The company has spent $30,000 on a report by a team of consultants, who have prepared the following estimates of the annual profit for each year of the project.

Year	1	2	3	4	5	6
Profit (in $'000)	60	75	100	60	40	20

What is the payback period for the project, to the nearest month?

☐ 2 years 7 months
☐ 2 years 10 months
☐ 4 years 2 months
☐ 4 years 11 months

8.19 A contract is to be commenced immediately. In one year's time it will require material EH. The material costs $7,800 now but will cost $8,800 in one year's time. The cost of storing EH for one year is $110 payable in one year's time.

If the contractor's cost of capital is 10% per annum, what is the present value of using the material if the contractor wishes to maximise profit?

☐ $7,900
☐ $7,999
☐ $7,800
☐ $7,910

8.20 **What would be a valid approach when calculating the NPV of a project which is subject to inflation?**

i Discount actual (nominal) cash flows at money discount rates
ii Discount actual (nominal) cash flows at real discount rates
iii Discount real cash flows at nominal discount rates
iv Discount real cash flows at real discount rates

☐ (i) only
☐ (ii) only
☐ (ii) and (iii)
☐ (i) and (iv)

8.21 Banbridge Ltd is about to carry out net present value analysis on a project. If the project is undertaken, a machine will be used that cost $300,000 when it was purchased 2 years ago and has a current written down value of $250,000. If the project is not undertaken, the machine could either be sold for $150,000 or used for another purpose. If it is used for another purpose, the company will be spared the cost of acquiring a new machine for $220,000. However, some improvements to the existing machine, costing $20,000, will be necessary.

What is the relevant cost of the machine when calculating the net present value of the project?

$ ☐

8.22 A company has a real cost of capital of 6% per annum and inflation is currently 4% per annum.

The company's annual money cost of capital is closest to:

- ☐ 10.24%
- ☐ 10%
- ☐ 2%
- ☐ 1.92%

8.23 K Ltd are considering an investment of $1,300,000. The company requires a minimum real rate of return of 10% under the present and anticipated conditions. Inflation is expected to be 3% per annum over the life of the investment and all costs and revenues are expected to increase in line with inflation.

Which of the following is the most appropriate approach to take to a DCF appraisal?

- ☐ Increase costs and revenues at 3% per annum and discount at 10%
- ☐ Make no adjustment to the cash flows for inflation and discount at 10%
- ☐ Increase the cash flows by 3% per annum and discount at 13%
- ☐ Make no adjustment to the cash flows for inflation and discount at 13%

8.24 **What is the present value of $1,500 costs incurred each year from years 3–6 when the cost of capital is 4%?**

- ☐ $4,680
- ☐ $5,034
- ☐ $4,500
- ☐ $3,700

9 Further aspects of decision making

9.1 A company is considering four capital projects in which to invest. All of the projects are divisible, which means that if the company invests in a fraction of a project, it will earn that fraction of the expected returns. Information about the projects is as follows:

Cash flows	Project W $	Project X $	Project Y $	Project Z $
Year 0	(10,000)	(8,000)	(18,000)	(17,000)
Year 1	3,000	7,000	0	0
Year 2	6,000	5,000	18,000	27,000
Year 3	8,000	3,000	15,000	–
Year 4	8,000	2,000	1,000	–
PV of annual cash profits	17,340	13,200	24,500	25,860

If there is capital rationing in Year 0, and none of the project start times can be delayed beyond year 0, how would the four projects be ranked in order of priority, starting with the most desirable project first?

- ☐ W, X, Y then Z
- ☐ W, X, Z then Y
- ☐ X, W, Z then Y
- ☐ Z, Y, W then X

9.2 Four investment projects are under consideration. Details are as follows.

Project	Year 0 outlay $'000	PV of future cash flows $'000	Profitability index $'000
A	200	300	1.50
B	600	800	1.33
C	1,000	1,300	1.30
D	1,600	1,800	1.125

Projects A and B are mutually exclusive. Projects C and D are mutually exclusive.

If the projects are divisible, but investment funds are restricted to $1,000,000, which projects should be undertaken?

☐ Project A and 80% of Project C
☐ Project A and 50% of Project D
☐ Project B and 40% of Project C
☐ Project B and 25% of Project D

9.3 Four products Red, Yellow, Green and Blue are available for development by a company which is facing shortages of capital over the current year but expects capital to be freely available from then on.

Project	Red $'000	Yellow $'000	Green $'000	Blue $'000
PV of total capital required over product's life	200	250	165	100
PV of capital required in current year	100	250	150	100
PV of sales receipts from products	375	650	435	310

In what order of preference should the products be developed?

☐ Red, Blue, Yellow, Green
☐ Yellow, Green, Blue, Red
☐ Green, Yellow, Red, Blue
☐ Blue, Green, Red Yellow

9.4 **When deciding between mutually exclusive investment projects with unequal lives, the decision should be based on a comparison of:**

☐ The net present value of future cash flows of each cycle
☐ The future value of future cash flows of each cycle
☐ Total cash flows of each cycle
☐ Annualised equivalent cash flows of each cycle

9.5 **When choosing between mutually exclusive projects with unequal lives on the basis of lowest annualised equivalent cost, we usually ignore which three of the following?**

☐ Annual running costs
☐ Future changes in cost of capital
☐ Future changes in technology
☐ That the product is unlikely to be produced forever
☐ Replacement costs

9.6 JKL plc has $1 million available for investment. It has identified three possible investments, J K and L, which each have a life of three years.

The three-year period coincides with JKL plc's investment plans.

JKL plc uses a 15% cost of capital when appraising investments of this type.

Details of these investments are set out below:

	J $'000	K $'000	L $'000
Initial investment	400	500	300
Net positive cashflows			
Year 1	40	70	50
Year 2	80	90	50
Year 3	510	630	380
Net present value	31	43	31

Assuming that each of the investments is divisible, they are not mutually exclusive and cannot be invested in more than once, state the optimum investment plan for JKL plc.

Project	Priority for funding (1-3)	Outlay $'000
J	☐	☐
K	☐	☐
L	☐	☐

9.7 A company has appraised three capital investment projects, and has produced the following analysis.

Project	Capital outlay $'000	PV of net cash flows $'000	NPV of project $'000	Profitability index
Alpha	480	1,050	570	2.19
Beta	600	1,200	600	2.00
Gamma	800	1,650	850	2.06

Given that capital available is restricted to $1,120,000, what is the maximum total NPV achievable, assuming that all three projects are divisible?

☐ $850,000
☐ $1,170,000
☐ $1,250,000
☐ $1,420,000

9.8 Four investment projects are under consideration. Details are as follows.

Project	Year 0 outlay $'000	PV of future cash flows $'000	Profitability index $'000
A	200	300	1.50
B	600	800	1.33
C	1,000	1,300	1.30
D	1,600	1,800	1.125

Projects A and B are mutually exclusive. Projects C and D are mutually exclusive.

If the projects are divisible and investment funds are not in restricted supply, which projects should be undertaken?

☐ Projects A and C
☐ Projects A and D
☐ Projects B and C
☐ Projects B and D

9.9 An investor is indifferent between replacing a machine every two years, and replacing it every four years.

The present value of the first 2 years replacement cycle is $17,360, and the present value of the first 4 year replacement cycle is $31,700.

What discount rate is the investor using?

☐ 5%
☐ 10%
☐ 15%
☐ 20%

9.10 **Complete the sentences using the following words below.**

- wait
- abandon
- follow on

An electronics company makes radios and is considering launching a new portable version which will give the company a competitive advantage for three years. They would need to buy new capital equipment for $400,000 which would have a scrap value of $60,000 in three years time. Launching the radio would give the company opportunity to launch further models at a later date. This is an option to [   ]. The opportunity to sell the capital equipment provides an option to [   ].

9.11 **What is the annual equivalent cost of spending a present value of $24,870 every 3 years if the discount rate is 10%?**

(use discount factors to three decimal places)

$ [   ]

9.12 A company is considering its asset replacement policy for a machine that it uses in its operations. The machine costs $15,000 and has a maximum expected useful life of 4 years. The expected annual running costs and the expected residual value of the machine are as follows.

	Running costs ($)	End of	Residual value ($)
Year 1	2,000	Year 1	7,000
Year 2	6,000	Year 2	4,000
Year 3	8,000	Year 3	1,000
Year 4	9,000	Year 4	0

The decision facing the company is whether to replace the machine annually, or every two, three or four years. The cost of capital is 15%.

Year	Discount factor at 15%	PV of $1 per annum	Discount factor at 15%
1	0.87		
2	0.76	Years 1 - 2	1.63
3	0.66	Years 1 - 3	2.29
4	0.57	Years 1 - 4	2.86

What is the equivalent annual cost of replacing the machine every 3 years, to the nearest $1,000?

$ [   ]

9.13 **Capital rationing is best described as a situation where:**

☐ A company has insufficient cash to undertake all the projects available to it

☐ A company has chosen to pay some of its cash to pay a dividend rather than undertaking all the projects that have a positive NPV at its cost of capital

☐ A company has insufficient projects available with a positive NPV to use up all its cash

☐ A company has insufficient cash to undertake all the projects that have a positive NPV at its cost of capital

---

9.14 A machine costing $150,000 has a useful life of eight years, after which time its estimated resale value will be $25,000. Annual running costs will be $5,000 for the first three years of use and $8,000 for each of the next five years. All running costs are payable on the last day of the year to which they relate.

Using a discount rate of 20%, what would be the annual equivalent cost of using the machine if it were bought and replaced every eight years in perpetuity (to the nearest $100)?

☐ $46,600
☐ $43,900
☐ $43,300
☐ $21,100

9.15   A company has recently developed a new lawnmower with an estimated market life of five years. Production and sale of the new lawnmower will require investment in new production equipment costing $750,000. It is expected that this equipment could be sold back to the original vendor for $50,000 at the end of 5 years.

Purchase of the equipment would be financed by a 5 year fixed rate bank loan at an interest rate of 6%.

A manager already employed by the company would be moved from his current position to manage production of the new lawnmower. His position would be filled by a new recruit on a fixed annual salary of $35,000.

Which of these statements is incorrect?

☐   If the lawnmower is a failure then management can terminate the project early and sell the equipment giving them an abandonment option.

☐   The salary of the replacement manager is a relevant cash flow in the decision.

☐   The interest costs on the bank loan are a relevant cash flow in the decision.

☐   Launching a new lawnmower gives an opportunity to launch more new versions and provides a follow on option.

☐   High frequency, high severity risks are often strategic risks.

9.16   A company expects to have spare production capacity during the coming three years and its directors are considering whether to undertake a contract for a fixed price of $1,000,000. Work on the new contract would have to start immediately and would take three years to complete. The management accountant has calculated that the NPV of the contract's cash flows is negative.

Which of the following statements is correct?

(i)   A negative NPV means that an investment proposal should always be rejected.

(ii)   The reliability of the data provided needs to be considered.

(iii)   The project can be considered in isolation without considering other projects.

(iv)   The effect on employees, customers' reaction and the flexibility of the business all need to be considered.

☐   (i), (ii), (iii)
☐   (i), (ii), (iii), (iv)
☐   (i), (iii)
☐   (ii), (iv)

9.17   **Use the words below to complete the following paragraph.**

- large
- insufficient
- positive
- external
- internal
- inappropriate

Capital rationing arises when there is ☐ capital to invest in all available projects which have

☐ NPVs. Hard rationing is where ☐ limits exist on funds available. Soft rationing is

where ☐ constraints are imposed.

9.18 An investment project that requires an initial investment of $500,000 has a residual value of $130,000 at the end of 5 years. The project's cash flows have been discounted at the company's cost of capital of 12% and the resulting net present value is $140,500.

The profitability index of the project is closest to:

- ☐ 0.02
- ☐ 0.54
- ☐ 0.28
- ☐ 0.26

10 Management control and risk

10.1 Briggs plc has analysed a particular risk faced by its Scarborough division on a risk map. It has concluded that the matter has a low impact but there is a high probability of its occurrence.

Which of the following risk responses would be most appropriate?

- ☐ Risk avoidance
- ☐ Risk reduction
- ☐ Risk transfer
- ☐ Risk acceptance

10.2 Daily sales of product X by Y Ltd are likely to be 400 units, 500 units or 600 units. The probability of sales of 500 units is 0.5, while the probability of sales of 600 units is 0.1.

Calculate the expected value of the daily sales volume.

| | units
|---|

10.3 A company manufactures mobile phones; it has two factories.

30% of the mobile phones are made in factory X, the other 70% in factory Y.

10% of factory X's production has a major fault, 12% of factory Y's production has such a fault.

A customer has just purchased a mobile phone that has a major fault.

What is the probability that it was made in factory Y?

| | % (give your answer to one decimal place)
|---|

10.4 **Which of the following is not a technique for measuring risk?**

- ☐ Sensitivity analysis
- ☐ Risk mapping
- ☐ Variance
- ☐ Standard deviation of expected returns

10.5 Claire Ltd is considering a project with the following revenue stream:

Year	Investment $'000	Variable costs $'000	Sales $'000	Net cash flows $'000
0	(10,000)			
1		(4,000)	9,000	5,000
2		(4,000)	9,000	5,000
3		(4,000)	9,000	5,000

The company's cost of capital is 5%.

By what percentage will sales have to fall for the project to produce a zero net present value?

- ☐ 14.8%
- ☐ 26.6%
- ☐ 33.2%
- ☐ 36.2%

10.6 Grenville Ltd is renewing its buildings and contents insurance policy covering its eight UK factories.

In terms of risk management, this is an example of:

- ☐ Risk avoidance
- ☐ Risk reduction
- ☐ Risk transfer
- ☐ Risk retention

10.7 A company has estimated the selling prices and variable costs of one of its products as follows:

Selling price per unit

$	Probability
40	0.30
50	0.45
60	0.25

Variable cost per unit

$	Probability
20	0.55
30	0.25
40	0.20

Given that the company will be able to supply exactly 1,000 units of its product each week irrespective of the selling price, and variable costs per unit are independent of each other, calculate the probability that the weekly contribution will exceed $20,000.

☐ %

10.8 Risk mapping is a technique for assessing the severity of a risk and the probability or frequency of its likely occurrence.

For what type of risk would it probably be most appropriate to take out an insurance policy from an insurance company?

- ☐ Severity high, frequency high
- ☐ Severity high, frequency low
- ☐ Severity low, frequency low
- ☐ Severity low, frequency high

10.9 X Ltd can choose from three mutually exclusive projects. The projects will each last for one year only and their net cash inflows will be determined by the prevailing market conditions. The forecast annual cash inflows and their associated probabilities are shown below:

Market Conditions	Poor	Good	Excellent
Probability	0.20	0.50	0.30
	$'000	$'000	$'000
Project L	500	470	550
Project M	400	550	570
Project N	450	400	475

Based on the expected value of the net cash inflows, which project should be undertaken?

☐ L

☐ M

☐ N

10.10 A 5-year project has a net present value of $160,000 when it is discounted at 12%. The project includes an annual cash outflow of $50,000 for each of the 5 years. No tax is payable on projects of this type.

The percentage increase in the value of this annual cash outflow that would make the project no longer financially viable is closest to:

☐ 64%

☐ 89%

☐ 113%

☐ 156%

10.11 **Which ONE of the following statements concerning Big Data is correct?**

☐ Big Data enables companies to mitigate risk.

☐ Big Data is often out of date before it can be used.

☐ Big Data is only relevant to short-term decisions.

☐ Big Data cannot be used to predict consumer preferences.

10.12 A company wishes to decide on a selling price for a new product.

Weekly sales of each product will depend on the price charged and also on customers' response to the new product. The following pay-off table has been prepared.

	Probability	Price P1	Price P2	Price P3	Price P4
		$	$	$	$
Price		5.00	5.50	6.00	6.50
Unit contribution		3.00	3.50	4.00	4.50
Weekly demand		Units	Units	Units	Units
Best possible	0.3	10,000	9,000	8,000	7,000
Most likely	0.5	8,000	7,500	7,000	6,000
Worst possible	0.2	6,000	5,000	4,000	3,000

If the choice of selling price is based on a maximax decision rule, which price would be selected?

☐ P1

☐ P2

☐ P3

☐ P4

10.13 **The main purpose of sensitivity analysis is to:**

☐ Predict the future outcome from an uncertain situation
☐ Determine the outcome from a situation in the event of the worst possible outcome
☐ Determine the expected value of an outcome that is uncertain
☐ Gain insight into which assumptions or variables in a situation are critical

---

10.14 A company wishes to decide on a selling price for a new product. Weekly sales of each product will depend on the price charged and also on customers' response to the new product. The following pay-off table has been prepared.

	Probability	Price P1	Price P2	Price P3	Price P4
		$	$	$	$
Price		5.00	5.50	6.00	6.50
Unit contribution		3.00	3.50	4.00	4.50
Weekly demand		units	units	units	units
Best possible	0.3	10,000	9,000	8,000	7,000
Most likely	0.5	8,000	7,500	7,000	6,000
Worst possible	0.2	6,000	5,000	4,000	3,000

If the choice of selling price is based on a maximin decision rule, which price would be selected?

☐ P1
☐ P2
☐ P3
☐ P4

10.15 The following statements have been made about decision making under conditions of uncertainty.

1. The expected NPV of a project is the value expected to occur if an investment project with several possible outcomes is undertaken once.

2. A risk-averse decision maker avoids all risks in decision making.

3. Expected values are used to support a risk-averse attitude to decision making.

4. Expected values are more valuable as a guide to decision making where they refer to outcomes which will occur many times over.

Which of the above statements is / are true?

☐ All of them
☐ 1, 3 and 4 only
☐ 1 and 2 only
☐ 4 only

10.16 A company wishes to decide on a selling price for a new product. Weekly sales of each product will depend on the price charged and also on customers' response to the new product. The following pay-off table has been prepared.

	Probability	Price P1 $	Price P2 $	Price P3 $	Price P4 $
Price		5.00	5.50	6.00	6.50
Unit contribution		3.00	3.50	4.00	4.50
Weekly demand		units	units	units	units
Best possible	0.2	10,000	9,000	8,000	7,000
Most likely	0.5	8,000	7,500	7,000	6,000
Worst possible	0.3	6,000	5,000	4,000	3,000

If the choice of selling price is based on the expected value decision rule, which price would be selected?

☐ P1
☐ P2
☐ P3
☐ P4

10.17 A company wishes to decide on a selling price for a new product. Weekly sales of each product will depend on the price charged and also on customers' response to the new product. The following pay-off table has been prepared.

	Probability	Price P1 $	Price P2 $	Price P3 $	Price P4 $
Price		5.00	5.50	6.00	6.50
Unit contribution		3.00	3.50	4.00	4.50
Weekly demand		units	units	units	units
Best possible	0.3	10,000	9,000	8,000	7,000
Most likely	0.5	8,000	7,500	7,000	6,000
Worst possible	0.2	6,000	5,000	4,000	3,000

If the choice of selling price is based on a minimax regret decision rule, which price would be selected?

☐ P1
☐ P2
☐ P3
☐ P4

10.18 **Which of the following are true in respect of using expected values in net present value calculations?**

1. Appropriate for one-off events
2. Hides risk
3. Probably won't actually occur
4. Eliminates uncertainty

☐ 1, 2 and 3 only
☐ 3 and 4 only
☐ 2 and 3 only
☐ 1, 2 and 4

10.19 The following financial information relates to an investment project:

	$'000
Present value of sales revenue	50,025
Present value of variable costs	25,475
Present value of contribution	24,550
Present value of fixed costs	18,250
Present value of operating income	6,300
Initial investment	5,000
Net present value	1,300

What is the sensitivity of the net present value of the investment project to a change in sales price?

☐ 7.1%

☐ 2.6%

☐ 5.1%

☐ 5.3%

10.20 **Which of the following statements is the main advantage of using simulations to assist in investment appraisal?**

☐ Statement 1 - simulation gives a clear decision rule.

☐ Statement 2 - with simulation, more than one variable can change at a time.

☐ Statement 3 - simulation is statistically more accurate than other methods.

☐ Statement 4 - being diagrammatic makes simulation easier to understand.

10.21 Helen Ltd has budgeted the following results for the year:

Sales	Probability
Units	
20,000	0.2
30,000	0.5
40,000	0.3

Sales price per unit is $20. Variable costs per unit are budgeted as follows.

Costs	Probability
$	
12	0.1
14	0.6
16	0.3

Fixed costs will be $175,000.

What is the probability that Helen will make a loss?

$ [ ]

10.22 Lynn Ltd has budgeted the following results for the year:

Sales Units	Probability
20,000	0.3
30,000	0.4
40,000	0.3

Sales price per unit is $20.

Variable costs per unit are budgeted as follows.

Costs $	Probability
12	0.2
14	0.5
16	0.3

Fixed costs will be $175,000.

What is the expected loss that Lynn will make?

$ [   ]

10.23 Efficiency and effectiveness are two key reasons for the introduction of information systems into an organisation.

Identify the three examples of efficiency from those below.

☐ Automation is pursued because a company expects it to help increase market share or satisfy customer needs.

☐ The speed of processing is improved.

☐ The cost of a computer system is lower than the manual system it replaces, mainly because the jobs previously performed by human operators are now done by computers.

☐ The accuracy of data / information and processing is improved, because a computer is less likely to make mistakes.

☐ Front office systems are developed to improve the organisation's decision-making capability.

10.24 Data and information come from sources both inside and outside an organisation.

Which three of the following represent data or information captured from within the organisation?

☐ Information about personnel from the payroll system
☐ Information on new employment legislation from the company secretary
☐ Value of sales from the accounting records
☐ Information on decisions taken from the minutes of a meeting
☐ Market information on buying habits of potential customers from the marketing manager

---

10.25 **Which of the following statements is true?**

☐ High frequency, high severity risks are always strategic risks.
☐ Risk transfer means the management of a portfolio of different risks.
☐ Insuring risks means that businesses will not need to take any measures to reduce those risks.
☐ Risk hedging is taking action to offset one risk by incurring a new risk in the opposite direction.

10.26 A project has a net present value of $320,000.

The sales revenues for the project have a total pre-discounted value of $900,000 and a total present value of $630,000 after tax.

The sensitivity of the investment to changes in the value of sales is closest to:

☐ $310,000

☐ $580,000

☐   51%

☐   36%

10.27 A project has an initial investment of $140,000 and a net present value of $42,500. The present value of the sales revenue generated by the project is $385,000.

The sensitivity of the investment to changes in the value of sales revenue is closest to:

☐   36%

☐ $342,500

☐   89%

☐   11%

10.28 **CIMA's Code of Ethics for professional accountants is based upon:**

☐   A framework of fundamental principles

☐   A framework of strict rules

☐   A scale of penalties for non compliance

☐   Sustainability principles and best practice

10.29 **Which two of the following statements are correct?**

☐   The value of perfect information is the difference between the EV of profit with perfect information and the EV of profit without perfect information.

☐   The value of perfect information is the difference between the EV of profit with imperfect information and the EV of profit without the information.

☐   The value of perfect information is the difference between the EV of profit with perfect information and the EV of profit with the imperfect information.

☐   The value of imperfect information is the difference between the EV of profit with imperfect information and the EV of profit without the information.

Answers to
objective test questions

1 Cost analysis and TQM

1.1 The correct answers are:

- It is dependent upon a close and mutually beneficial working relationship with suppliers.
- It can result in much reduced inventory holding costs.
- It requires suppliers to operate sound quality control procedures.

The aim of JIT is to increase efficiency of inventory control systems in order to reduce company costs, principally by minimising inventory levels and thus stockholding costs. This is achieved by using reliable suppliers who can deliver goods of the right quality in the right quantity at the right time. The burden of quality control is generally passed back to the supplier to cut costs of the company.

JIT works best when a tied supplier relationship is formed, where the orders form a large part, if not the entirety, of the supplier's business. This precludes the use of many different suppliers. In a JIT system, steps will also be taken to improve customer relations and communications, so that demand can be more accurately determined. This means that reorder levels, and thus safety inventories, can be minimised without necessarily increasing the risks (and thus costs) of stock outs.

1.2 The correct answer is: $7.50.

Step 1

Cost driver is number of batches, therefore calculate number of batches for each product and in total.

	X	Y	Z	Total
Production units	15	25	20	
Batch size	2.5	5	4	
Number of batches	6	5	5	16

Step 2

Calculate machine set-up costs attributable to product Y using number of batches as the allocation basis.

Machine set up costs $\dfrac{5}{16} \times 600{,}000 = \$187{,}500$

Step 3

Calculate the machine set-up costs that would be attributable to each unit of Product Y:

Machine set up costs	= $187,500
Production units	= 25,000
Machine set-up costs per unit	= $7.50

1.3 The correct answer is: All of the above.

External failure costs are costs arising outside the manufacturing organisation of failure to achieve a specified quality (after transfer of ownership to the customer).

1.4 The correct answer is: I, II and III.

Issue I WCM aims to know what customer requirements are, to supply customers on time and to change products / develop new products as customers need change.

Issue II As above, WCM aims to change products / develop new products as customer needs change.

Issue III WCM incorporates the principles of TQM.

Issue IV Attempting to recover overheads through production could lead to excess stocks and possibly of unwanted products. This is not a strategy of WCM.

1.5 The correct answer is: I, II and III.

I: Due to low inventory levels, any disruption in supply will impact the production process.

II: JIT, originated by Toyota, was designed at a time when all of Toyota's manufacturing was done within a 50 km radius of its headquarters.

III: JIT is not suitable for all organisations, particularly those where demand is unpredictable

IV: Because stocks are held at minimum level, there is very little risk that they might become obsolete.

1.6 The correct answer is: Eliminate the costs of poor quality.

TQM aims to eliminate the costs of poor quality – not just reduce them. It is not possible to eliminate all quality-related costs without ceasing production. TQM does not aim to reduce the workforce – although changes in working methods may be required to improve quality.

1.7 The correct answer is: Customer X.

This is even though X receives a higher discount as the analysis below shows:

	Customer X	Customer Y
	$	$
Revenue	16,000	20,000
Less discount	2,400	2,000
Net revenue	13,600	18,000
Less:		
cost of items (at $20 each)	8,000	10,000
transport costs	–	4,000
admin costs	400	200
Net gain	5,200	3,800
Number of units sold	400	500
Net gain per unit sold	13.00	7.60
Net gain per $1 of revenue	0.33	0.19

1.8 The correct answer is: Equipment maintenance is a product / process level cost.

Such costs are caused by the development, production or acquisition of different items.

1.9 The correct answer is: Material costs as throughput.

The theory of constraints focuses on factors such as bottlenecks which act as constraints to this maximisation.

1.10 The correct answers are:

- Employees are often viewed as the cause of problems.
- It is used for cost control.

Employees are viewed as the source of (and are empowered to find) solutions. Kaizen costing is used for cost reduction – not cost control. The other options all relate to Kaizen costing.

1.11 The correct answer is: $47,500.

The correct cost driver for set-up costs is the number of production runs. There are a total of 100 production runs across the three products and therefore there is a cost of $950 per production run ($95,000 / 100). There are 50 production runs allocated to Product X and therefore the allocated set-up cost to Product X is 50 x $950 = $47,500.

1.12 The correct answer is: $24.50.

Overhead allocation to Product A.

Set-up costs: $40,000

Number of production runs = 100 (35 + 40 + 25)

Set-up cost per production run = $40,000 / 100 = $400

Set-up costs allocated to Product A = $400 × 35 = $14,000

Inspection costs: $37,500

Number of inspections = 75 (15 + 25 + 35)

Inspection costs per inspection = $37,500 / 75 = $500

Inspection costs allocated to Product A = $500 × 15 = $7,500

Inventory handling costs: $13,500

Number of inventory requisitions = 45 (10 + 15 + 20)

Inventory requisition cost per requisition = $13,500 / 45 = $300

Inventory requisition costs allocated to Product A = $300 × 10 = $3,000

Total overheads allocated to Product A = $24,500 ($14,000 + $7,500 + $3,000)

Total overheads per unit = $24.50 ($24,500 / 1,000)

1.13 The correct answer is: (a), (b), (d) and (e) only.

ABM includes cost reduction, product design decisions, operational control and performance evaluation.

Although there have been a great many different definitions of ABM, none have specifically included variance analysis.

ABM does include more than the activities mentioned above, however.

1.14 The correct answer is: I and III only.

ABC is regarded as an improvement for reasons I and III. All overheads are addressed under traditional absorption methods.

1.15 The correct answer is: IV only.

IV is a feature of traditional absorption costing methods.

1.16 The correct answer is: III only.

ABC is sometimes introduced because it is fashionable, not because it will be used by management to provide extra information, to alter the production mix or to control non-value-added activities.

I: ABC is particularly useful in an advanced manufacturing technology environment where overhead costs are a significant proportion of total costs.

II: This provides a means of controlling the occurrence of the overhead cost.

IV: ABC recognises the complexity of manufacturing with its multiple cost drivers.

1.17 The correct answer is: A factor which causes the costs of an activity.

A factor which causes the costs of an activity is the correct description of a cost driver. It is the factor which causes the costs of an activity to increase or decrease. For example, a cost driver for materials handling costs could be the number of production runs: the higher the number of production runs, the higher the cost of material handling will be.

1.18 The correct answer is: All of them.

I: JIT requires close integration of suppliers with the company's manufacturing process.
II: In other words, JIT requires the use of machine cells.
III: JIT recognises machinery set-ups as a non-value-adding activity.
IV: Each component on a production line is produced only when needed for the next stage.

1.19   The correct answer is: I, III and IV.

   I: Short-term variable overhead costs vary with the volume of activity, and should be allocated to
         products accordingly.

   II: This statement is not completely correct. Many overhead costs, traditionally regarded as fixed costs,
         vary in the long run with the volume of certain activities, although they do not vary immediately. The
         activities they vary with are principally related to the complexity and diversity of production, not to
         sheer volume of output. For example, set-up costs vary in the long run with the number of production
         runs scheduled, not the number of units produced.

   III: For example, the number of credit investigations undertaken within the credit review department of a
         bank would be the cost driver of the department's costs.

   IV: Following on from III above, a mortgage might require three credit investigations and hence the
         mortgage should bear the proportion of the departments' costs reflected by three credit investigations.

1.20   The correct answer is: Just-in-time.

   Producing or purchasing items as they are needed is referred to as Just-in-Time (JIT).

1.21   The correct answer is: I and III.

   Rule I was first suggested by the economist Pareto in the context of the distribution of wealth. It is only very
   approximately observed in practice.

   There is no such general guidance to the effect of **rule II.**

   Rule III was initially suggested by the economist Pareto on the basis of his observations of social inequality.

   Rule IV is incorrect because, according to the 80 / 20 rule, the richest 20% of the population owns 80% of the
   wealth, compared to only 20% owned by the rest of the population.

2   Techniques for enhancing long-term profits

2.1   The correct answer is: Neither 1 nor 2.

   Cam Co's target costing system may take product development costs into consideration, but recovery of
   product design and development costs is associated more with life cycle costing. Even with life cycle costing,
   recovery of design and development costs is not ensured: much depends on whether customers will buy
   enough webcams at the target price.

   In target costing, a cost gap is the difference between the current estimate of the cost per webcam and the
   target cost that the Cam Co wants to achieve.

2.2   The correct answers are:

   •   Cost value
   •   Exchange value
   •   Use value
   •   Esteem value

   Incremental and target values are not related to value analysis.

2.3   The correct answer is:

   •   Quality function deployment identifies customer requirements and ensures that these drive product
       design and process planning.

   Value engineering is the application of value analysis to **new** products.
   Functional analysis is applied during the **development** stage of a new product.
   Value analysis aims to improve quality **without** increasing costs.

BPP
LEARNING MEDIA

2.4   The correct answer is: 10.

Required profit = 20 × 20% = 4

Target cost = 20 − 4 = 16

Current cost = 26 − 16 = 10

2.5   The correct answer is:

The value chain is the sequence if business activities by which **value** is added to an organisation's products and services. The **primary** activities include inbound and outbound **logistics**, marketing and sales and **operations**. The **support** activities include human resource management, firm infrastructure and **procurement**. A firm is profitable if the value perceived by customers is greater than the **cost** of activities that create that perception.

2.6   The correct answers are:

- Using standard components wherever possible
- Acquiring new, more efficient technology

To make improvements towards the target cost, technologies and processes must be improved.

The use of standard components is a way of improving the production process.

Redundancy creates short-term costs such a redundancy pay-offs, may affect the long-term morale of the group and, if it leads to the organisation being under resourced, may affect the quality of the product and customer service.

Reducing the quality may lead to a loss of business and competitiveness.

2.7   The correct answer is: $15.40.

	$
Projected revenue (200,000 × $25)	5,000,000
Desired profit (0.12 × $16m)	1,920,000
Total target cost	3,080,000
Unit target cost ($3,080,000 / 200,000)	$15.40

2.8   The correct answer is: Functional analysis is concerned with functions, perceived value and cost.

Functional analysis is concerned with improving profits by attempting to reduce costs and / or by improving products by adding new features in a cost-effective way that are so attractive to customers that profits actually increase due to an increase in perceived value.

2.9   The correct answer is: Value analysis can result in both the elimination and reduction of costs and may also increase sales.

The aim of value analysis is to eliminate unnecessary costs without reducing the value of the product in the eyes of the customer. Such exercises may actually help increase sales volumes if the price of the product can be reduced as a consequence of reduced costs.

2.10   A food producer produces one type of low cost food and production techniques have remained largely unchanged for a number of years. It has been struggling with falling sales. The company could improve its position by adopting **kaizen costing**. This is applied during the manufacturing stage of the **lifecycle** and focuses on achieving **incremental** improvements. This type of costing is based on the assumption that the manufacturing process is always able to **improve**.

2.11   The correct answer is: Market price minus desired profit margin.

Target cost means a product cost estimate derived by subtracting a desired profit margin from a competitive market price.

2.12   The correct answer is: A competitive market price.

2.13   The correct answer is: $38.

Required return	= 12% × $900,000	
	= $108,000	
Expected revenue	= 4,000 × $65	
	= $260,000	
Therefore total target cost	= $(260,000 − 108,000)	
	= $152,000	
Therefore unit target cost	= $152,000 / 4,000	
	= $38	

2.14   The correct answer is: Procurement and Human resource management.

These are support services in the value chain. Operations and service are primary activities.

2.15   The correct answer is: ii and iv.

Target costing focuses on costs at the development stage.

Kaizen costing is applied during the manufacturing stage.

2.16   The correct answer is: Inbound logistics involves the storing of finished goods

2.17   The correct answer is: The cost gap is calculated as the estimated product cost minus the target cost.

2.18   The correct answer is: $0.40.

Target profit (25% of cost = 20% of sales price) = $2

Target cost $10 − $2 = $8

Target cost gap = $8.40 − $8 = $0.40

2.19   The correct answer is: all of the above costs.

Direct product costs include warehouse direct costs, transport direct costs and store direct costs.

3   Cost planning

3.1   The correct answer is: 7.53 minutes.

$Y = aX^{-0.3219}$

a = 18 minutes

If the cumulative number of units (X) = 5, the cumulative average time per unit (Y) = $18 \times 5^{-0.3219}$ = 10.722

∴ Total time for 5 units = 10.722 × 5 = 53.61 minutes

If the cumulative number of units (X) = 4, the cumulative average time per unit (Y) = $18 \times 4^{-0.3219}$ = 11.520

∴ Total time for 4 units   = 11.520 × 4   = 46.08 minutes

∴ Time for fifth unit   = 53.61 − 46.08   = 7.53 minutes

3.2   The correct answer is: At the design / development stage.

The bulk of a product's life cycle costs will be committed at the design / development stage (being designed in at the outset during product and process design, plant installation and setting up of the distribution network). At this point the business will have committed to incurring the majority of the product's lifecycle cost.

3.3   The correct answers are:

- Planning and concept design costs
- Preliminary and detailed design costs
- Testing costs
- Production costs
- Distribution and customer service costs

Life cycle costs are incurred from design stage through to withdrawal from the market.

3.4   The correct answer is: $560.

Average time per unit for first two units	= 100 × 90%	90 hours
∴ Total time taken for first two units	= 90 × 2	180 hours
Less time taken for first unit		100 hours
Time taken for second unit		80 hours
Labour cost at $7 per hour		$560

3.5   The correct answers are:

- A relatively new product
- A manual, rather than mechanised production process
- A relatively complex production process

If a product is relatively new it means that workers are still learning.

If a process is manual (as opposed to one that is mechanised), learning can reduce the time taken.

If the production process is relatively complex there are processes and techniques to learn.

Production can be in batches of any size – equal sizes just make the calculations easier.

Changing labour rates do not affect the application of learning curve theory.

3.6   The correct answer is: 15.22.

The formula for the learning curve is $Y_x = aX^b$

So Y_{16} $= 54 \times 16^{-0.3219}$

            $= 22.12$

Y_{16} $= 54 \times 15^{-0.3219}$

            $= 22.58$

Remember that these are average times for each stage and not the incremental time to produce an extra unit.

Cumulative units	Average time / unit	Total time
	hours	hours
15	22.58	338.70
16	22.12	353.92
Incremental time for the 16th unit		15.22

3.7   The correct answer is: 83.5%.

The approach to derive the learning rate very much depends on the information given in the question. If you are provided with **details about cumulative production levels of 1, 2, 4, 8 or 16 (etc) units** you can use the **approach** shown below.

Let the rate of learning be r:

Cumulative production	Cumulative average time
	Hours
1	3
2	$3 \times r$
4	$3 \times r^2$

∴ $3r^2$ = 8.3667 / 4

r^2 = 2.092 / 3 = 0.697

r = 0.835

∴ The rate of learning is 83.5%

3.8 The correct answers are:

- When products are made by a highly mechanised process
- When products are made in small quantities for special orders

Machines do not learn, and a relatively large quantity of the product must be made in order for significant repetition and learning to occur.

3.9 The correct answer is: The profiling of cost over a product's development, production life and dismantling period.

LCC looks at costs only, but over the product's whole life cycle.

3.10 The correct answer is: $12,492.

With a 70% learning curve, the cumulative average time per unit of output will fall to 70% of what it was each time output is doubled.

No. of items		Cu. Ave. time per item		Total time for all items to date
1		600	(x1)	600
2	(x70%)	420	(x2)	840
4	(x70%)	294	(x4)	1176

Therefore the price for the first 4 items is:

	$
Materials	24,000
labour (1,176 hrs at $6 per hr)	7,056
Overhead (150% of labour)	10,584
Total cost	41,640
Profit mark-up 20%	8,328
Total sales price for 4 items	49,968
Price per item	12,492

3.11 The correct answer is: Life cycle costing is the profiling of costs over a product's production life.

It also includes development costs and so on, prior to production, and any costs, such as dismantling costs after production has ceased.

All the other statements are true.

3.12 The correct answer is: Maturity stage.

During the introduction stage, brand awareness needs to be built. Advertising needs to be stepped up during the growth stage to build brand preference. Promotional expenditure is reduced during the decline stage and focuses on reinforcing the brand image of remaining products in the product line.

3.13 The correct answer is: To gain consumer preference and increase sales.

During the introduction stage, the aim is to establish a market and build demand.

During the maturity stage, the aim is to maintain market share and extend the product's life cycle.

3.14 The correct answer is: Growth.

The information requirements can be summarised as follows:

Introduction: Basic quality, few competitors, no economies of scale, high promotion costs.

Growth: As stated

Maturity: Most competitive stage, product extension strategies eg. new markets, product offspins.

Decline: Exit strategy needs to be identified.

3.15 The correct answer is: $8,503.

$a = 25$

$b = -0.1520$

$x = 64$

$y = ax^b$

$y = 25 \times 64^{-0.1520}$

$y = 13.286$

Total cost $= 13.286 \times 64 \times \$10 = 8503$.

3.16 The correct answer is: $28,056.

Average cost per batch of 4 batches	$= 40,000 \times 4^{-0.152}$	$= \$32,400$
Total cost for 4 batches	$= 32,400 \times 4$	$= \$129,601$
Total cost for 3 batches	$= 3 \times 40,000 \times 3^{-0.152}$	$= \$101,545$
Cost for 4th batch	$= 129,600 - 101,544$	$= \$28,056$

3.17 The correct answer is: 85%.

$a = 1,562.5$

$Y_{16} = 12,800 / 16 = 800$

Learning rate $= 4\sqrt{(800 / 1562.5)} - 1 = 0.8459$

3.18 The correct answer is: Life cycle costing.

Benchmarking is not a cost management tool.

Kaizen costing focuses on cost reduction during the production stage of a product's life cycle.

Target costing focuses particularly on cost reduction during the planning, research and design stages of the life cycle.

3.19 The correct answer is: None of the above.

Reducing material costs or increasing the sales price will increase throughput per machine hour. Reducing factory costs will reduce the factory cost per machine hour. These will increase the TA ratio.

4 Pricing

4.1   The correct answer is: $300.

a = 1,000

b = 1 / 50

Profit maximising price = a − bx

P = 1,000 − (1 / 50 × 35,000)

P = 300

4.2   The correct answer is: $1,365.

$$b = \frac{\text{change in price}}{\text{change in quantity}} = \frac{\$1}{5} = 0.2$$

a = $250 + ((12,000 / 5) × $1) = $2,650

MR = 2,650 − (2 × 0.2)Q   = 2,650 − 0.4Q

Profits are maximised when MC = MR, ie when 80 = 2,650 − 0.4Q

To work out value for Q:

0.4Q = 2,650 − 80

Q = 2,570 / 0.4 = 6,425

Therefore, profit-maximising demand (Q) = 6,425

Now, substitute the values into the demand curve equation to find the profit-maximising selling price

P = a − bQ

P = 2,650 − (0.2 × 6,425)

∴ Profit-maximising price = $(2,650 − 1,285) = $1,365

4.3   The correct answer is: Minimum pricing is based on relevant costs.

A minimum price is the price that would have to be charged so that the incremental costs of producing and selling an item plus the opportunity costs of the resources consumed in making and selling it are just covered.

Marginal cost plus pricing is also known as full cost plus pricing is false. Marginal cost plus pricing is also known as mark-up pricing.

Full cost plus pricing is used for profit maximisation is false. Full cost plus pricing fails to recognise that since demand may be determined by price, there will be a profit-maximising combination of price and demand.

Demand is a main factor in the full cost plus approach to pricing is false. Full cost plus pricing does not recognise the economic relationship between price and demand.

4.4   The correct answer is:

A company manufactures and sells a number of products all of which have a life cycle if six months or less. It has recently developed an innovative product and has decided to launch it with a high price initially as the product is **unique**. This is a market **skimming** pricing strategy which will allow the company to gain high profits **early** in the product's lifecycle. In the growth stage, selling prices are likely to **decrease**.

4.5   The correct answer is: By $2 per unit.

When P = 24 – 0.004Q, the marginal revenue MR = 24 – 0.008Q

Total sales revenue increases when the price is increased as long as the marginal revenue is a positive value.

MR starts to go into negative values when sales demand exceeds the quantity where:

24 – 0.008Q = 0

Q = 3,000

At this demand quantity, the sales price is P = 24 – 0.004 (3,000) = $12.

The company can raise the sales price by $2 to $12 per unit in order to increase sales revenue, but at higher prices total sales revenue will fall.

(Check: If P = $12 and Q = 3,000, total weekly revenue = $3,600. This is $100 per week more than the revenue from selling 3,500 units at $10 each.)

4.6   The correct answer is: $35.

Marginal cost = $20

Profits are maximised when marginal cost = Marginal revenue

ie when 20   = 50 – 0.002x

ie when x   = 15,000

When x = 15,000, selling price = $50 – $(0.001 × 15,000) = $35

4.7   The correct answer is: $8.40.

P = a – bQ / DQ

b = 1

DQ = 2,500

a = 12 + (16,000 × 1) / 2,500 = 18.4

So P = 18.4 – Q / 2,500

To sell 25,000 tickets,

P = 18.4 – 25,000 / 2,500 = $8.40 per ticket

4.8   The correct answer is: If demand is highly elastic.

If demand is highly elastic it responds well to low prices.

If a product is new and different, market skimming would be more appropriate. Customers would be prepared to pay high prices so as to be one up on other people who do not own the product.

Market penetration pricing is appropriate if there are significant economies of scale to be achieved from a high volume of output, so that quick penetration into the market is desirable in order to gain unit cost reductions.

4.9   The correct answer is: When the product is expected to have a long life cycle.

Market skimming is an appropriate pricing policy when a product is expected to have only a short life cycle; prices need to be set at a high level in order to recover development costs quickly and maximise short-term profit.

The protection of a patent creates a barrier to entry to the market for competitors and enables the holder of the patent to charge higher prices than would otherwise be possible. When demand is unknown it is probably safer to charge a higher price, to improve the chance of recovering development costs and making a profit.

4.10   The correct answer is:

b   =   15 / 1,000
P   =   a − bx
735 =   a − (0.015 × 1,000)
a   =   735 + 15   = 750
MR =   750 − 0.03x
MC =   42 + 7.9   = 49.9
MR =   MC
750 =   750 − 0.03x   = 49.9
x   =   (750 − 49.9) / 0.03 = 23,337
P   =   750 − (0.015 × 23,337) = 399.95

4.11   The correct answer is: $317.

Profit is maximised at seven units of output and a price of $317, when MR is the closest to MC.

4.12   The correct answer is: P = 523 − Q / 250.

P = a − bQ / change in Q and a = current price + $b (current quantity at current price/change in quantity when price is changed by $b). In this instance, a = $95 + $10(107,000 / 2,500) = $523. The demand curve is therefore P = 523 − 10Q / 2,500 = 523 − Q / 250.

4.13   The correct answer is $24.50.

P = a − bx

b = 1 / 100 = 0.01

P = $25

x = 1,000

25 = a − (0.01 × 1,000)

a = 25 + 10

a = 35

Marginal Revenue (MR) = a − 2bx

MR = 35 − 0.02x

Marginal cost (MC) = $14

So if MC = MR then:

14 = 35 − 0.02x

0.02x = 21

x = 1,050 units

Substituting x = 1,050 in the demand function to find price:

Optimal selling price = $35 - (0.01 × 1,050) = $24.50 per unit.

4.14 The correct answer is: A strategy of penetration pricing could be effective in discouraging potential new entrants to the market by charging a low price when the product is first launched whereas the strategy of market skimming is to gain high unit profits early in the products life cycle, thus allowing the costs of developing the product to be recovered.

Penetration pricing is a strategy that is often used in the introduction phase of a product's life cycle. A low price is charged to penetrate an existing market when the product is first launched to gain market share.

Market skimming is a strategy that is mainly used in the introduction phase of the product life cycle when the product is unique, technologically advanced. A high price can be charged at launch in order to recover the research and developments costs already incurred.

Penetration pricing is a policy of charging low prices when the product is first launched in order to obtain sufficient penetration in the market whereas market skimming is a policy of charging high prices when a product is first launched and attracting customers through heavy advertising and sales promotion.

4.15 The correct answer is: Market skimming.

Charging a high price when the product is first launched to gain high unit profits early in the products life cycle, thus allowing the costs of developing the product to be recovered.

Penetration pricing is a strategy that is often used in the launch phase of a product's life cycle. A low price is charged to penetrate an existing market when the product is first launched to gain market share. Since the games console is a unique product this strategy would not allow the company to maximize profits. However, after six months when competitors enter the market, strategy can be changed to penetrate the market.

Dual pricing is an internal or transfer pricing strategy and not used for pricing products for external sales.

'Own label' pricing is used by supermarkets and retail stores who sell their 'own label' products, often at a lower price than established branded products. They do this by entering into arrangements with manufacturers, to supply their goods under the 'own brand' label. So this strategy will not apply to the games console.

4.16 The correct answer is: (i), (iii).

Factors other than price will also affect demand eg advertising, incomes.

Market skimming is often used for new and different products with a short product lifecycle.

4.17 The correct answer is: In the growth stage, costs are likely to be decreasing as costs are shared over more units.

4.18 The correct answer is: $215.

For every $1 change in price, the quantity demanded will change by 4,000/10 = 400 units

When demand Q = 0, the price will be: 180 + (50,000 / 400) = 305

Demand curve P = 305 − (1 / 400) × Q = 305 − 0.0025Q

Total revenue = 305Q − 0.0025Q$_2$

Marginal revenue = 305 − 0.005Q

Marginal cost = 125

Profit maximised when 305 − 0.005Q = 125, Q = 36,000

P = 305 − (0.0025 × 36,000) = $215

4.19 The correct answer is: $96.

An increase in price of $25 will result in a fall in demand quantity by 6,250 units. Each $1 change in price therefore results in a change in demand by 6,250 / 25 = 250 units.

Demand Q will be 0 when the price P is $145 + $(5,000 / 250) $165

Demand function = 165 − Q / 250 = 165 − 0.004Q

Marginal revenue = 165 − 0.008Q

Profit is maximised when marginal revenue equals marginal cost:

When $27 = 165 - 0.008Q$, so $Q = 138 / 0.008 = 17,250$

Price $= 165 - (17,250 / 250) = \$96$

4.20 The correct answer is: To increase the length of the initial stage of the life cycle.

Penetration pricing, by encouraging more customers to buy the product at an early stage in its life cycle, should shorten the length of the initial stage of the life cycle. As demand picks up, the product will enter into its growth stage more quickly.

5 Decision making in responsibility centres

5.1 The correct answer is: Recognises different cost behaviour patterns and is designed to change as the volume of activity changes.

A flexible budget is designed to change as the volume of activity changes.

5.2 The correct answer is: I only.

A flexible budget can be used to control operational efficiency.

Incremental budgeting takes last year's budget and adds an amount for estimated growth or inflation. Unplanned extra units of activity are accounted for once actual performance is being measured.

Rolling budgets are continuous budgets which extend the current budget as the current period ends.

5.3 The correct answer is: Attainable.

An attainable standard makes an allowance for normal inefficiencies but also includes hoped-for improvements. An ideal standard assumes an optimum level of efficiency. A current standard is based on current efficiency levels and achievements.

A basic standard is not updated regularly in order to shows change over the long term.

5.4 The correct answer is: $14,000.

Production units sold	8,000
Budget	$'000
Sales ((35 / 5) × 8)	56
Variable costs ((20 / 5) × 8)	32
Contribution	24
Fixed costs	10
Profit	14

5.5 The correct answer is: (top-down) budgets may not be realistic in practice.

When senior managers impose budgets on managers below them in the organisation hierarchy, there is a risk that the imposed budgets will be unrealistic because senior managers may not have a full understanding of operational realities.

5.6 The correct answer is: (ii) only.

Statement (i) is not correct. A fixed budget may be useful for control purposes where activity levels are not prone to change, or where a significant proportion of costs is fixed, so that alterations in activity levels do not affect the costs incurred.

Statement (ii) is correct. Fixed and variable costs must be separately identified so that the allowance for variable costs may be flexed according to the actual activity level.

Statement (iii) is not correct. Budgetary control procedures can be used to monitor and control income as well as expenditure.

5.7 The correct answer is: $264,000.

Administration costs are 100% fixed costs

	Production costs $'000	Selling costs $'000
Cost of 7,000 units	231	19
Cost of 5,000 units	(195)	(15)
Variable cost of 2,000 units	36	4
Variable cost per unit	$18	$2

	$'000	$'000
Total cost of 5,000 units	195	15
Variable cost of 5,000 units	(90)	(10)
Fixed costs	105	5

	$'000
Variable cost of making 6,000 units (× $18)	108
Variable cost of selling 5,500 units (× $2)	11
Fixed costs (105 + 35 + 5)	145
Total budgeted cost allowance	264

5.8 The correct answer is: Managers do not give budgeting enough of their time.

The BBRT believe that managers usually give budgeting too much of their time. They also propose that budgets protect rather than reduce costs because managers have a 'use it or lose it' mentality to spending their full budget expenditure allowance. They say budgets discourage innovation and initiative because managers are discouraged from taking actions that are 'not in the budget', and that budget targets are often driven by financial measures like sales targets, rather than more qualitative and ultimately more indicative measures like customer satisfaction.

5.9 The correct answers are: Use adaptive management processes rather than the more rigid annual budget. Move towards devolved networks rather than centralised hierarchies.

The two fundamental concepts of the Beyond Budgeting approach are the use of adaptive management processes rather than fixed annual budgets and a move to a more decentralised way of managing the business with a culture of personal responsibility.

5.10 The correct answer is: Both 1 and 2.

If the workforce knows in advance that the initial targets they are given will more than likely be revised (as the same thing happens every period) then there is a risk that they will start to ignore them.

A severe criticism of planning and operational variances is the lack of objectivity that may be involved in deciding in retrospect what the standard cost should have been.

5.11 The correct answer is:

A proportion of rent and rates for the building the production department shares with other departments.

Managers should only be held accountable for costs over which they have some influence.

5.12 The correct answer is: They do not take much time to prepare.

Generally they are time-consuming because significant co-ordination between units is needed.

5.13 The correct answer is: Maximising performance potentials.

The Beyond Budgeting® model uses adaptive processes and goals are based on maximising performance potentials.

5.14 The correct answers are:

- Managers may introduce budgetary slack.
- Managers may set easy budgets to ensure they are achievable.

As the managers are involved in the budget process and their performance judged against the budget, there is an incentive to make the budget as achievable as possible.

In general they are more realistic than imposed budgets and capture resource requirements. This is because the managers preparing the budget are most aware of the issues likely to be faced and the resources needed in the future.

5.15   The correct answer is: $61,640.

	$
Budgeted contribution at 400 units	53,600
Budgeted contribution per unit (53,600 / 400)	134
Flexed budgeted contribution (460 × 134)	61,640

5.16   The correct answer is: Participative.

Participative budgets are developed by lower-level managers who then submit the budgets to their superiors.

5.17   The correct answer is: Neither 1 nor 2 is correct.

There is likely to be a demotivating effect where an ideal standard of performance is set, because adverse efficiency variances will always be reported. It is important that adverse variances are not used to lay blame if targets have been set with the aim of motivation.

A low standard of efficiency is also demotivating, because there is no sense of achievement in attaining the required standards. Managers and employees will often outperform the standard or target when in fact they could have performed even better if they had been sufficiently motivated.

5.18   The correct answer is: deliberate overestimation of costs and / or underestimation of revenues in a budget.

In the process of preparing budgets, managers might deliberately overestimate costs and underestimate sales, so that they will not be blamed in the future for overspending and poor results. This is budget slack.

5.19   The correct answer is: Goal congruence in decision making.

There is a risk of dysfunctional decision making and a lack of goal congruence with divisionalisation. Divisional managers may base investment decisions on whether they will improve ROI, which is inappropriate. Transfer pricing disputes too may lead to bad decisions by divisional managers. However, the risk can be avoided or minimised if divisional management and head office management are aware of the potential problem.

Authority is delegated to divisional managers; therefore there is some loss of head office control over operations, but decision making at 'local' operational level should be faster since the decision does not have to be referred to head office for a decision. There is likely to be some duplication of costs, since each division will have its own administration activities.

6 Performance measurement

6.1 The correct answer is: Diagnostic.

Diagnostic benchmarking involves reviewing the processes of a business to identify those which indicate a problem and offer a potential for improvement. For example, a company may critically assess each element of the value chain and conclude that there is potential for improvement within the marketing and sales function.

Competitive benchmarking involves comparing internal performance with that of (successful) competitors

Metric benchmarking is the practice of comparing appropriate metrics to identify possible areas for improvement. For example, IT investment as a percentage of total assets may be compared across different departments within the same company to identify areas of the company where additional investment is required.

Process benchmarking is the practice of comparing processes with a partner as part of an improvement process. For example, a distributor of personal computers may analyse a competitor's supply chain function in the hope of identifying successful elements of the process that it can use to its advantage.

6.2 The correct answer is: ROI – yes, RI – yes.

The ROI target is 10% and the cost of capital is 9%. The ROI is calculated as ($15,000/$100,000) × 100% = 15% and so the project should be accepted and would be accepted because the ROI is greater than the target.

The RI is calculated as $15,000 – (9% × $100,000) = $6,000. The project should be accepted and would be accepted because the RI is positive.

6.3 The correct answer is: 2.16m.

	$m
Current profit (($21m × 16%) + $0.8m)	4.16
Imputed interest (($25m × 8%)	(2.00)
Residual income	2.16

6.4 The correct answer is (i), (ii), and (iii).

Statement (i) is the formula for calculating EVA®

Statement (ii) is correct. Economic profit is derived by making a series of adjustments to the accounting profit, such as adjusting historic accounting depreciation and adding back any 'investment expenditure' such as advertising or R & D.

Statement (iii) is perceived to be an advantage of EVA® as it will not lead to sub-optimal decisions with respect to new investment as it is the absolute increase in shareholder value which is used as a criterion.

6.5 The correct answer is: Environmental perspective.

The missing perspective is the innovation and learning perspective, or 'can we continue to improve and create value'?

6.6 The correct answer is: 23.5%.

The divisional return on investment $= \dfrac{\text{Operating profit before interest}}{\text{Total assets less current liabilities}}$

$$= \frac{400}{2{,}100 - 400} \times 100$$

$$= 23.5\%$$

The profit is stated before interest so that we can assess the division's effectiveness in using all of its assets, irrespective of how these assets are financed. We are told that all decisions concerning the division's capital structure are taken by central management. Finance costs and the way the assets are financed is therefore outside the control of the division. The denominator will therefore include all sources of funds (equity and long term borrowings) and the numerator will be the operating profit before the deduction of attributable finance costs.

6.7 The correct answer is: $196,000.

$400 - (1{,}700 \times 12\%) = \$196{,}000$

6.8 The correct answer is: ROI – no, RI – no.

The current ROI	= ($1,700,000 / $5,000,000) × 100	= 34%
The new ROI	= ($(1,700,000 + 75,000) / $(5,000,000 + 150,000 + 350,000)) × 100%	= 32.3%

The project would therefore be rejected because the ROI would fall.

The current RI	= $1,700,000 – (18% × $5,000,000)	= $800,000
The new RI	= $(1,700,000 + 75,000) – (18% × $5,500,000)	= $785,000

The project would therefore be rejected because the RI would fall.

6.9 The correct answer is: $24.84 million.

The concept of EVA is that the economic profit of a business must exceed the cost of capital invested.

EVA = Net operating profit after tax – Capital charge on the replacement cost of assets.

The relevant rate is the division's risk adjusted cost of capital of 11%.

Although not explicitly stated in the question we need to make the assumption that the new product was launched at the beginning of the year and therefore one third of the launch costs need to be amortised over the period. We also need to assume that the unamortised launch costs are not included in the replacement cost of assets ($172m) and therefore need to be added on.

EVA = NOPAT – Capital charge

= ($40.2m + $6m – $2m) – (11% × ($172m + $4m))

= $44.2m – $19.36m   = $24.84m

6.10 The correct answer is: 44.

ROCE = (Operating profit / Capital employed) × 100%

= (3,629,156 / (4,582,000 + 4,619,582 + 442,443 – 949,339 – 464,692)) × 100%

= 44% rounded down

6.11 The correct answer is: Innovation and learning.

Developing new products is clearly related to innovation.

6.12 The correct answer is: A learning and growth perspective.

A target of providing at least 40 hours of training every year to improve skills and productivity has a learning and growth perspective.

6.13   The correct answer is: (i) and (ii) only.

Percentage of on-time deliveries and customer complaints per month, (i) and (ii) would both be appropriate for monitoring the customer perspective because they both represent targets that would matter to customers.

Monitoring of the average set-up time (iii) would be more appropriate from the internal perspective. It focuses on improving internal processes but is not directly important to the customer.

6.14   The correct answer is: How well the assets of a business are used to generate sales.

Asset turnover = sales / capital employed.

6.15   The correct answer is: Delivery time.

The other options are all financial performance measures.

6.16   The correct answer is: 3.

Profit margin = PBIT / Sales = 27,500 / 550,000 = 0.05 = 5%

Profit margin $\times$ asset turnover = ROCE

Therefore:

5% $\times$ asset turnover = 15%

Asset turnover = 15% / 5% = 3.

6.17   The correct answer is: Competitive.

Competitive benchmarking involves comparing performance with direct competitors, often through analysing their products or services.

6.18   The correct answer is: - $577,500.

RI = $300,000 − $6.75 million $\times$ 13% = $300,000 − $877,500 = - $577,500

6.19   The correct answer is: 4.44%

$$ROI = \frac{300,000}{6,750,000} \times 100 = 4.44\%$$

6.20   The correct answer is: Internal business (operational) perspective.

The target is to improve the efficiency of dealing with customer calls. This may affect customer satisfaction and profitability, but its prime objective is to reduce call times and improve efficiency in the call centre.

7   Transfer pricing

7.1   The correct answer is: Both 1 and 2.

Internal transfers should usually be preferred to external purchases because the company will have better control over output quality from Division A and the scheduling of production and deliveries. Transfer prices determine how total profit will be shared between the divisions.

7.2 The correct answers are:

Budgeted profit / (loss) for Division Y when the transfer price is set at marginal cost $(1,000)

Budgeted profit / (loss) for Division Y when the transfer price is set at the total production cost $1,400

(i) Budgeted loss – marginal cost transfer price

		$'000
Sales		
Internal	60,000 × $100	6,000
External	40,000 × ($150 × 1.3333)	8,000
		14,000
Variable cost	100,000 × $100	10,000
Contribution		4,000
Fixed costs		
Production	100,000 × $40	4,000
Administration	100,000 × $10	1,000
Loss		(1,000)

(ii) Budgeted profit – absorption cost transfer price

		$'000
Sales		
Internal	60,000 × $140	8,400
External	40,000 × ($150 × 1.3333)	8,000
		16,400
		10,000
Variable cost	100,000 × $100	10,000
Contribution		6,400
Fixed costs		
Production	100,000 × $40	4,000
Administration	100,000 × $10	1,000
Profit		1,400

7.3 The correct answers are:

- Because there is often no external market for the product that is being transferred
- Because the external market is imperfect

If there is no external market there will be no suitable market price upon which to base the transfer price.

If the external market is imperfect, the market price will be affected by factors such as the amount that the company setting the transfer price supplies to it or limited external demand.

The transferring division will want to maximise its profits but this is not a reason for using cost-based approaches to transfer pricing.

The buying division will want to maximise its profits but this is not a reason for using cost-based approaches to transfer pricing.

7.4 The correct answer is: $19 per unit.

RI = Annual profit – (Cost of capital × Capital employed)

$200,000 = Annual profit – (10% × 3,600,000)

Annual profit = 200,000 + 360,000

Annual profit required to achieve the RI target = $560,000

Annual profit = External sales revenue + Internal sales revenue – Variable costs – Fixed costs.

560,000 = ((200,000 - 60,000) × $33) + (60,000 × P) – (200,000 × $20) – $1,200,000

560,000 = 4,620,000 + 60,000P – 4,000,000 – 1,200,000

P = (4,000,000 + 1,200,000 – 4,620,000 + 560,000) / 60,000

P = $19

7.5 The correct answer is: $33 and $20.

External sales demand is 160,000 Units. Maximum capacity is 200,000 Units so by transferring 60,000 units to Division B, external sales of 20,000 Units are lost.

The opportunity cost-based transfer price of these 20,000 Units = variable cost + contribution lost from not selling externally.

This equals $20 + $13 = $33 = the external selling price.

The remaining 40,000 Units can be produced using spare capacity, so the transfer price of these Units equals their variable cost ie $20.

7.6 The correct answer is $182,000.

Division X contribution will be:

	$'000	
Contribution: from external sales	170	
from sales to Y	12	(1,000 units)
	182	

7.7 The correct answer is: $11.50.

A profit margin of 20% on transfer prices equates to a 25% mark-up on costs.

	X $ per unit	Y $ per unit	Z $ per unit
Transfer cost	–	30.00	62.50
Added materials	8.00	6.00	6.00
Direct labour	6.00	4.00	8.00
Production overhead	10.00	10.00	12.00
Full cost	24.00	50.00	88.50
Profit per unit	6.00	12.50	11.50
Transfer price per unit	30.00	62.50	100.00

Profit per unit = $100 – 88.50 = $11.50.

7.8 The correct answer is: $14.

Contribution from external sales per unit = $(16 – 10 – 2) = $4 and so the company will prefer internal sales if the contribution per unit on internal sales is greater than $4. The variable cost per unit is $10 and so the transfer price should be $14 (the market price less variable selling costs).

7.9 The correct answer is: Reduce the level of fixed costs.

It may not be possible for the supplying division to reduce its fixed costs, and even if it does its unlikely to be able to reduce them to zero, so some will always remain unrecovered. The other measures suggested could help the supplying division to recover all of its fixed costs.

7.10 The correct answer is: It is not possible to tell without further information.

If Q uses the external supplier, P loses the contribution of $18 ($52 – $34) per unit. The group saves costs of $34 per unit but pays $49 per unit, and so group profit is reduced by $15 per unit.

However, we do not know whether division P is able to sell component X externally, nor whether the division has spare capacity. If division Q purchases externally it may be possible for division P to expand profits, for the division and for the group, by selling externally.

Therefore it is impossible to tell the effect on profit without further information.

7.11   The correct answer is: $132,400.

If B buys from A:

A's revenue	140,000 × $33	4,620,000
	60,000 × $20.20	1,212,000
A's costs	(200,000 × $20)	(4,000,000)
Net cash flow		1,832,000
Tax at 50%		916,000
		916,000
B's costs	60,000 × $20.20	1,212,000
30% tax allowed against this		363,600
		848,400
Net position for Group		67,600

IF B buys from W:

A's revenue	160,000 × $33	5,280,000
A's costs	(160,000 × $20)	(3,200,000)
Net cash flow		2,080,000
Tax at 50%		1,040,000
		1,040,000
B's costs	60,000 × $20	(1,200,000)
30% tax allowed against this		360,000
		(840,000)
Net position for Group		200,000

7.12   The correct answer is: It enables profit centres to make entirely autonomous decisions.

A task of head office is to try to prevent dysfunctional decision-making by individual profit centres. To do this, head office must reserve some power and authority for itself and so profit centres cannot be allowed to make entirely autonomous decisions.

7.13   The correct answers are:

- When variable costs and market prices are constant
- When a perfect external market exists

If variable costs and market prices are constant, regardless of the volume of output, a market based transfer price is the ideal transfer price.

If a perfect external market exists, market price is the ideal transfer price.

7.14   The correct answers are:

- Less than or equal to the selling price minus variable costs in the receiving division
- Greater than or equal to the variable cost in the supplying division

This transfer price will enable performance to be measured fairly as both divisions will at least cover their variable costs.

7.15   The correct answer is: $6.00.

Managers of each division will also be willing to increase output (above the budget) provided that it is profitable to do so.

(a)   The manager of M will increase output if the transfer price exceeds the variable cost of $4 a unit.

(b)   The manager of S will increase output if the transfer price is less than the difference between the fixed selling price ($14) and the variable costs in S itself. This amount of $9 ($14 - $5) is sometimes called net marginal revenue.

The range of prices is therefore between $4.01 and $8.99.

7.16   The correct answers are:

- As an incentive to control costs
- The supplying division is being assessed as a profit centre

Using market value will force the supplying division to manufacture at a unit cost below this threshold, or else it will appear loss-making.

If the market price is subject to wide fluctuations then this is a good reason **not** to use it as a transfer price as the instability will lead to difficulties in administering the transfer pricing system and / or uncertainty in how to interpret divisional performance.

If there is no external market then there will not be a robust market value on which to base the transfer price. For example, if the component transferred is being made only for a specific company product.

7.17   The correct answer is: The message sent to the supplying division is that fixed costs must be controlled.

A two-part tariff system can be used to ensure that the selling division's fixed costs are covered. Transfer prices are set at variable cost and there is a periodic transfer of a fixed fee to the supplying division (representing an allowance for fixed costs).

However the risk is that the supplying division does not control its fixed costs because the company will subsidise inefficiencies.

7.18   The correct answer is: Goal congruence. This is a consideration for all companies, and is not exclusive to multinational companies.

Taxation: Different tax rules and rates in different countries can affect the transfer pricing decision. For example, it may be possible to adjust the transfer price to reduce the taxable profit in countries where tax rates are high. Although governments tend to take action to try to stop this happening, it is a consideration to be borne in mind when setting international transfer prices.

Anti-dumping legislation: Governments may take action to protect their home industries by preventing companies from transferring goods cheaply into their countries. They may do this, for example, by insisting on the use of a fair market value for the transfer price.

Tariffs: When setting transfer prices, management must take account of the import tariffs applicable in the receiving countries. If the tariffs are based on the value of the import then it may be appropriate to set a low transfer price in order to reduce the tariff payable.

---

8   Project appraisal

8.1   The correct answer is: -$268.60.

The NPV = $((7,000) × 1,000 + $5,000 × 0.870 + $800 × 0.756 + $2,700 × 0.658) = -$268.60.

8.2   The correct answers are:

Both methods give the same accept or reject decision, regardless of the pattern of the cash flows	**False**
IRR is technically superior to NPV and easier to calculate	**False**
The NPV approach is superior if discount rates are expected to vary over the life of the project	**True**
NPV and accounting ROCE can be confused	**False**

(a)   The methods only give the same accept or reject decision when the cash flows are conventional. When the cash flow patterns are non-conventional, there may be several IRRs that decision makers must be aware of to avoid making the wrong decision.

(b)   On the contrary, NPV is technically superior to IRR and easier to calculate.

(c)   Variable discount rates can be incorporated easily into NPV calculations, but not into IRR calculations.

(d)   NPV is dissimilar to accounting ROCE, but IRR can be confused with ROCE since both measures are expressed in percentage terms.

8.3 The correct answer is: IRR = 10 + [(49/(49 - 18) × (15 − 10))] = 17.9%.

8.4 The correct answer is: 14%.

Using the IRR interpolation formula:

$$IRR = 0.10 + \left[\frac{12,304}{12,304 + 3,216} \times (0.15 - 0.10) \right] = 0.14 \text{ or } 14\%$$

8.5 The correct answer is 11.32%.

Using the relationship between the money rate and real rate of inflation.

$(1 + 0.18)$ = $(1 + x) \times (1 + 0.06)$

1.1132 = $1 + x$

0.1132 = x

To the nearest 0.01%, x = 11.32%

8.6 The correct answer is: None of the above.

I.   is not a disadvantage because the fact that it tends to bias in favour of short-term projects means that it tends to minimise both financial and business risk.

II.   is untrue. It is simple to calculate and simple to understand, which may be important when management resources are limited.

III.   is not a disadvantage because it helps to identify those projects which generate additional cash for investment quickly.

8.7 The correct answer is: $660,000.

Since we are given a money cost of capital, the actual money cash flows must be used in the appraisal:

Yr	Investment $	Fixed costs $	Contribution $	Net cash flow $	14% factor	Present value $
0	(700,000)			(700,000)	1.000	(700,000)
1		(200,000)	620,000	420,000	0.877	368,340
2		(210,000) (+ 5%)	663,400 (+7%)	453,400	0.769	348,665
3		(220,500) (+ 5%)	709,838 (+7%)	489,338	0.675	330,303
4		(231,525) (+ 5%)	759,527 (+7%)	528,002	0.592	312,577

Net present value 659,885
= $660,000 to the nearest $'000

8.8 The correct answer is: 4.4 years.

The **discounted payback** period is the **time it takes for a project's cumulative NPV to become positive**.

With a cost of capital of 10% and the cash flows shown below, we can calculate a discounted payback period.

Year	Cash flow $'000	Discount factor 10%	Present value $'000	Cumulative NPV $'000
0	(450)	1.000	(450)	(450)
1	130	0.909	118	(332)
2	130	0.826	107	(225)
3	130	0.751	98	(127)
4	130	0.683	89	(38)
5	150	0.621	93	55

The DPP is during year 5.

DPP = 4 + (38 / 93)

= 4.4 years

8.9 The correct answer is: 1.5 years.

Step 1

As payback is calculated using cash flows, we have to convert profits into cash flows by adding back depreciations.

Depreciation per annum = $\dfrac{\text{Cost} - \text{Residual Value}}{\text{Expected useful life}}$

$= \dfrac{400,000 - 50,000}{5} = \$70,000$

Year	Profit $	Depreciation $	Cash flow $
1	175,000	70,000	245,000
2	225,000	70,000	295,000
3	340,000	70,000	410,000
4	165,000	70,000	235,000
5	125,000	70,000	195,000

Step 2

Calculate payback period using the cash flows calculated in Step 1 above.

Year	Cash flow	Cumulative Cash flow
0	(400,000)	(400,000)
1	245,000	(155,000)
2	295,000	140,000

Payback is between one and two years. Use interpolation to obtain a more accurate answer:

Payback = $1 + \dfrac{155,000}{295,000}$ years

= 1.5 years (to nearest 0.1 years).

8.10 The correct answer is 12.50%.

Using the formula

IRR = 2 + (35,000 / (35,000 − 15,000) × (8 − 2)) = 12.5%

8.11 The correct answer is: $4,981

The net present value of the annuity is 26,496, hence:

26,496	= ($a × AF$_{1-4}$)+10,000	Where AF$_{1-4}$ is the 4 year 8% annuity factor
16,496	= $a × 3.312	(from tables)
$a	= 16,496 / 3.312	
	= $4,981 (rounded up)	

8.12 The correct answer is: $223,400.

The present value of the holiday home = $1.5m × (DF$_5$10%) = $1.5m × 0.621 = $931,500

Therefore the present value of the annuity = $931,500.

931,500 = $a × AF$_{0-4}$

Where AF$_{0-4}$ is the annuity factor from time 0 to time 4

AF$_{0-4}$ = 1 + AF$_{1-4}$	= 1 + 3.170 = 4.170	
So 931,500	= $a × 4.170	
$a	= 931,500 / 4.170	
	= 223,381 or $223,400 to the nearest $100	

8.13 The correct answer is: $5,625.

Year 20X0 – Plant cost = $100,000

WDA claimed (25%) = $100,000 × 0.25 = $25,000

WDA value carried forward to 20X1 = $75,000 ($100,000 – $25,000)

WDA claimed = $18,750 ($75,000 × 0.25)

Tax saved = $5,625 ($18,750 × 0.3)

8.14 The correct answer is: MIRR is calculated on the basis of investing the inflows at the cost of capital.

The statement is correct. The others are incorrect. The central bank's cost of capital is irrelevant to MIRR. MIRR takes into account capital outflows as well as inflows. Future cashflows are discounted.

8.15 The correct answer is: 12%.

Year	0	1	2	3	4
Cash flow	24,500	15,000	15,000	3,000	-3,000
Compound factors (Reinvested at CoC 10%)		1.331	1.21	1.1	1
Compounded Value to T4		19,965	18,150	3,300	-3,000

Terminal Value $= 19,965 + 18,150 + 3,300 - 3,000 = 38,415$

Total Return (terminal/outlay) $= \dfrac{38,415}{24,500} = 1.57959$

Annual Return (MIRR) $= \left(\sqrt[4]{1.567959}\right) - 1$

$= 0.119099$ or 11.9%

Rounded to 12%

8.16 The correct answer is: Before depreciation but after taxation.

The returns should be calculated before depreciation but after taxation. Taxation is a cash flow, depreciation is not.

8.17 The correct answer is: Initial cost of the investment outlay.

The internal rate of return is therefore the rate of return at which the project's net present value is zero.

8.18 The correct answer is: 2 years 7 months. Annual depreciation on the equipment would be $(300,000 – 60,000) / 6$ years = $40,000. Annual cash flows will be the profit plus depreciation.

Year	Cash flow $'000	Cumulative $'000
0	(300)	(300)
1	100	(200)
2	115	(85)
3	140	55

Payback = 2 years + (85 / 140) × 12 months = 2 years 7 months.

8.19 The correct answer is: $7,900.

If the contractor buys the material now, the present value of the cost is $(7,800 + ($110 × 0.909) = $7,900.

If he buys it in a year's time, the present value of the cost is $8,800 × 0.909 = $7,999.

The contractor should choose the lower of the two as he wishes to maximise profit.

8.20 The correct answer is: (i) and (iv).

We can either discount actual (nominal) cash flows at nominal discount rates or discount real cash flows at real discount rates.

8.21 The correct answer is: $200,000.

The best alternative use for the machine is to use it for another purpose, saving a net $220,000 – $20,000 = $200,000, rather than selling it for $150,000. The project should thus be charged with the cost of this lost opportunity.

8.22 The correct answer is: 10.24%

$$1+ \text{money cost of capital} = (1+ \text{real cost of capital})(1+ \text{inflation rate})$$

$$= (1 + 0.06)(1 + 0.04)$$

$$= 1.1024$$

Money cost of capital is 10.24%.

8.23 The correct answer is: Make no adjustment to the cash flows for inflation and discount at 10%

If the cash flows are expressed in constant price level terms, the real rate of 10% is used as the discount factor.

8.24 The correct answer is $5,034.

The PV of $1,500 in costs each year from years 3 to 6 when the cost of capital is 4% per annum is calculated as follows.

$$\$1,500 \times \begin{bmatrix} \text{PV of \$1 per annum for years } 1-6 \text{ at } 4\% = 5.242 \\ \text{Less PV of \$1 per annum for years } 1-2 \text{ at } 4\% = 1.886 \\ \text{PV of \$1 per annum for years } 3-6 \qquad = 3.356 \end{bmatrix}$$

PV = $1,500 × 3.356 = $5,034

If you chose $4,680, you performed the calculation $1,500 × 104% × 3 years. You need to use a discount factor.

If you chose $4,500, you simply took the sum of $1,500 paid annually for 3 years.

If you chose $3,700, you deducted the cumulative discount factor for years 1 to 3 instead of the factor for years 1 and 2 from that for years 1 to 6.

---

9 Further aspects of decision making

9.1 The correct answer is: W, X, Z then Y.

Divide the PV of annual cash profits by the year 0 outlay to find the profitability index.

	Project W	Project X	Project Y	Project Z
PV of annual cash profits	$17,340	$13,200	$24,500	$25,860
Year 0 outlay	$10,000	$8,000	$18,000	$17,000
Profitability index	1.734	1.65	1.361	1.521
	1st	2nd	4th	3rd

9.2 The correct answer is: Project A and 80% of Project C.

Since capital is rationed to $1,000,000, the aim should be to maximize the present value of future cash flows per $1 invested.

Choice	Higher profitability index	Outlay required $
Projects A or B	Project A (1.50)	200,000
Projects C or D	Project C (1.30)	1,000,000
		1,200,000

Only $1,000,000 is available and as Project A has a higher profitability index than Project C, the company should choose 100% of Project A and 80% (1,000,000 – 200,000/1,000,000) of Project C.

9.3 The correct answer is: Blue, Green, Red, Yellow.

The company should aim to maximize present value of net flows per $1 of outlay in Year 0, the year that capital is rationed. As there are cash outflows after year 0, net present value has been used in the calculation.

Project	PV of future cash flows after year 0	NPV	Current Year capital outlay		
Red	375 – 200	175	100	1.75	3
Yellow	650 – 250	400	250	1.60	4
Green	435 – 165	270	150	1.80	2
Blue	310 – 100	210	100	2.10	1

9.4 The correct answer is: Annualised equivalent cash flows of each cycle.

Remember, we can only compare the net present values (or future values) of future cash flows if all the projects have equal lives.

9.5 The correct answers are:

- Future changes in the cost of capital
- Future changes in technology
- That the project is unlikely to be produced forever

Our calculations do reflect annual running costs and replacement costs

9.6 The correct answers are:

Project	Priority for funding (1-3)	Outlay $'000
J	3	200
K	2	500
L	1	300

Project	Investment required $'000	Present value of cash inflows* $'000	NPV $'000	Profitability index (PI)**	Ranking as per NPV	Ranking as per PI
J	400	431	31	1.08	=2	3
K	500	543	43	1.09	1	2
L	300	331	31	1.10	=2	1

However, only $1 million is available for capital investment.

* NPV + initial investment

** PV of cash inflows/PV of total capital outlay

As projects are divisible, it is possible to invest fully in projects L and K, with the remaining balance of $200,000 being invested in J (so one half of the full investment would be made to earn one half of the NPV).

Project	Priority	Outlay $'000		NPV
L	1st	300		31
K	2nd	500		43
J (balance)	3rd	200	(½ of $31,000)	15
		1,000		89

9.7 The correct answer is: $1,250,000.

Project	Profitability index	Amount of outlay $'000	NPV of inflows $'000
Alpha	2.19	480	570
Gamma	2.06	(bal)640	680
		1,120	1,250

NPV Gamma = 850 × 640 / 800 = 680

9.8   The correct answer is: Projects B and C.

As funds are not in short supply, net present value should be used to determine which projects to undertake.

Project B	has a higher net present value	(800 – 600 = 200)	than
Project A		(300 – 200 = 100),	and
Project C	has a higher net present value	(1,300 – 1,000 = 300)	than
Project D		(1,800 – 1,600 = 200).	

9.9   The correct answer is: 10%.

This item is best attacked by trial and error, using the costs of capital given in the question. For the investor to be indifferent, the annual equivalent costs must be the same.

At 10%, the annual equivalent costs are:

2 year cycle	= $17,360 / 1.736
	= $10,000
4 year cycle	= $31,700 / 3.170
	= $10,000

9.10 The correct answer is:

An electronics company makes radios and is considering launching a new portable version which will give the company a competitive advantage for three years. They would need to buy new capital equipment for $400,000 which would have a scrap value of $60,000 in three years time. Launching the radio would give the company opportunity to launch further models at a later date. This is an option to **follow on**. The opportunity to sell the capital equipment provides an option to **abandon**.

9.11 The correct answer is: $10,000.

To calculate the annual equivalent cost, divide the present value by the 3 year cumulative discount factor at 10%

ie $24,870 / 2.487 = $10,000

9.12 The correct answer is: $11,000.

The annual cash flows are the running costs less any income from the sale of the asset at the year end. The cash flows over a replacement cycle with each replacement option are as follows.

Year	Every year $	Every 2 years $	Every 3 years $	Every 4 years $
0	(15,000)	(15,000)	(15,000)	(15,000)
1	5,000	(2,000)	(2,000)	(2,000)
2		(2,000)	(6,000)	(6,000)
3			(7,000)	(8,000)
4				(9,000)

The PV of these cash flows, discounting at 15%, is as follows.

Year	Every year PV $	Every 2 years PV $	Every 3 years PV $	Every 4 years PV $
0	(15,000)	(15,000)	(15,000)	(15,000)
1	4,350	(1,740)	(1,740)	(1,740)
2		(1,520)	(4,560)	(4,560)
3			(4,620)	(5,280)
4				(5,130)
	(10,650)	(18,260)	(25,920)	(31,710)

	Every year $	Every 2 years $	Every 3 years $	Every 4 years $
PV of costs over replacement cycle	(10,650)	(18,260)	(25,920)	(31,710)
Discount factor	0.87	1.63	2.29	2.86
Equivalent annual PV of cost	$12,241	$11,202	$11,319	$11,087

9.13   The correct answer is: A company has insufficient cash to undertake all the projects that have a positive NPV at its cost of capital.

9.14   The correct answer is: $43,900.

NPV = -150,000 + (25,000 × 0.233) − (5,000 × 2.106) − (8,000 × 2.991 × 0.579) = -168,559

EAC = 168,559 / 3.837 = $43,930

9.15   The correct answer is: The interest costs on the bank loan are a relevant cash flow in the decision.

Finance costs are not included in the relevant cash flows. They will form part of the calculations for an appropriate discount rate.

9.16   The correct answer is: (ii), (iv).

A negative NPV does not always mean that an investment proposal should be rejected. There may be links with other projects and real options may be available.

Non-financial factors need to be considered.

9.17   The correct answers are:

Capital rationing arises when there is **insufficient** capital to invest in all available projects which have **positive** NPVs. Hard rationing is where **external** limits exist on funds available. Soft rationing is where **internal** constraints are imposed.

9.18   The correct answer is: 0.28.

The profitability index is stated as the NPV of a project/initial outlay.

NPV = $140,500 and initial outlay = $500,000.

Therefore the profitability index is $140,500 / $500,000 = 0.281 which is closest to 0.28.

---

10 Management control and risk

10.1   The correct answer is: Risk reduction.

Where a risk falls into the low impact, high probability quadrant of the risk map the most appropriate response is risk reduction, focusing on reducing the likelihood of the adverse event occurring.

10.2   The correct answer is: 470.

EV = (500 × 0.5) + (600 × 0.1) + (400 × (1 − 0.5 − 0.1)) = 470

10.3 The correct answer is: 73.7%.

$$P\left(\frac{A}{B}\right) = \frac{P(A) \times P(B \mid A)}{P(B)}$$

Where:

P(A) is the probability of A occurring

P(B) is the probability of B occurring

P(B|A) is the probability of B occurring given that A had occurred

Let:

P(A) = probability of a phone being made in Factory Y

P(B) = probability of a phone being faulty

So:

P(A) = 0.7

P(B) = (0.3 × 0.1) + (0.7 × 0.12) = 0.114

P(B|A) = 0.12

Therefore, given that a phone is faulty, the probability that is was made in Factory Y is

P(A|B) = (0.7 × 0.12) / 0.114 = 0.73684 or 73.7%

Workings using a contingency table:

Choosing 1,000 as a suitable multiple, ie considering 1,000 mobile phones are manufactured, the contingency table is:

	Factory X	Factory Y	Total
Has major fault	30	84	114
	(30% × 1,000 x 10%)	(70% × 1000 × 12%)	

Factory Y with a major fault = 84/114 = 73.7%

10.4 The correct answer is: Risk mapping.

Risk mapping is a technique for assessing risks, in terms of frequency and severity. It leads on to risk measurement, but is not itself a technique for measuring risk. Risks can be measured as (severity × frequency) or (impact × probability), for which techniques such as statistical analysis (for example standard deviation and variance) and sensitivity analysis can be used.

10.5 The correct answer is: 14.8%.

Current present value

Year		Cash flow $'000	Discount factor $'000	Discounted cash flows $'000
0	Investment	(10,000)	1.000	(10,000)
1-3	Receipts	9,000	2.723	24,507
1-3	Costs	(4,000)	2.723	(10,892)
				3,615

Therefore sales must reduce by 3,615 / 24,507 = 14.8%.

Alternative working

Discounted sales receipts 24,507 – 3,615 = $20,892

Annual sales receipts = 20,892 / 2.723 = $7,672

Reduction in sales receipts = 9,000 – 7,672 / 9,000 = 14.8%.

10.6 The correct answer is: Risk transfer.

Insurance transfers risk. In return for an insurance premium, the insurance company agrees to take on an agreed proportion of the financial burden of a risk.

10.7 The correct answer is: 44.75%.

This requires you to run through the different combinations of selling price and variable cost that will give a contribution exceeding $20,000 / week or $20 per unit.

Clearly at a selling price of $40 / unit all contributions of 1,000 units will be less than $20,000. So you should be able to eliminate a few combinations using this basic logic.

Thus the combinations of selling price and variable cost that give at least $20,000 and the probability resulting:

Selling price (unit) $	Variable cost $	Probability
50	20	0.45×0.55
60	30	0.25×0.25
60	20	0.25×0.55
		44.75%

10.8 The correct answer is: Severity high, frequency low.

Insurance might be the most appropriate risk hedging strategy when the potential cost is high, but the likelihood of the adverse outcome happening is fairly low. When the frequency is high, internal measures to manage the risk would probably be more appropriate.

10.9 The correct answer is: Project M.

EV of L   = $(0.2 \times \$500 + 0.5 \times \$470 + 0.3 \times \$550)$ = $500,000
EV of M   = $(0.2 \times \$400 + 0.5 \times \$550 + 0.3 \times \$570)$ = $526,000
EV of N   = $(0.2 \times \$450 + 0.5 \times \$400 + 0.3 \times \$475)$ = $432,500

Project M should be undertaken as it has the highest EV.

10.10 The correct answer is: 89%.

Sensitivity = (NPV of project / PV of variable) × 100

= ($160,000 / ($50,000 × 3.605)) × 100

= 88.77%

10.11 The correct answer is: Big Data enables companies to mitigate risk.

Risk can be mitigated where a company has high volumes of information. This is something that Big Data provides. It is relevant to long-term, as well as short-term decision making and is updated in real-time so is not out of date. It is often used to predict consumer preferences successfully.

10.12 The correct answer is: $6.00.

	Weekly contribution			
	Price P1 $	Price P2 $	Price P3 $	Price P4 $
Best possible	30,000	31,500	32,000	31,500

The maximax decision rule is to select the price offering the maximum possible benefit, which is P3. This will provide the biggest weekly contribution, provided that the best possible sales demand is achieved.

10.13 The correct answer is: Gain insight into which assumptions or variables in a situation are critical. Sensitivity analysis does not use probabilities so it does not predict outcomes (points 1-3 in the question).

However, because it identifies the variables that only have to change by a small percentage for the NPV of a project to fall to zero then it does identify the input variables that are most critical to the situation or decision.

10.14 The correct answer is: P1.

	Weekly contribution			
	Price P1	Price P2	Price P3	Price P4
	$	$	$	$
Worst possible	18,000	17,500	16,000	13,500

The maximin decision rule is to select the price offering the maximum possible benefit under the worst of circumstances. Price P1 will provide the biggest weekly contribution under the worst of circumstances, which is a contribution of $18,000 if the worst possible demand occurs.

10.15 The correct answer is: 4 only.

Expected values (EVs) are more valuable as a guide to decision making where they refer to outcomes which will occur many times over, because EVs represent a long-run expected average outcome.

Explanation of the incorrect statements.

1.   The second part of this statement is not true, it should say 'is undertaken many times'.
2.   A risk averse decision maker may minimise risk but cannot eliminate it.
3.   EVs support a risk-neutral attitude to decision making.

10.16 The correct answer is: P3.

	Prob	Price P1		Price P2		Price P3		Price P4	
		Cont'n	EV	Cont'n	EV	Cont'n	EV	Cont'n	EV
		$	$	$	$	$	$	$	$
Best	0.2	30,000	6,000	31,500	6,300	32,000	6,400	31,500	6,300
Most likely	0.5	24,000	12,000	26,250	13,125	28,000	14,000	27,000	13,500
Worst	0.3	18,000	5,400	17,500	5,250	16,000	4,800	13,500	4,050
Total EV			23,400		24,675		25,200		23,850

10.17 The correct answer is: P2.

	Weekly contribution			
	Price P1	Price P2	Price P3	Price P4
	$	$	$	$
Best possible	30,000	31,500	32,000	31,500
Most likely	24,000	26,250	28,000	27,000
Worst possible	18,000	17,500	16,000	13,500

	Regret vs best outcome under each scenario			
	Price P1	Price P2	Price P3	Price P4
	$	$	$	$
Best possible	2,000	500	0	500
Most likely	4,000	1,750	0	1,000
Worst possible	0	500	2,000	4,500
Maximum regret	4,000	1,750	2,000	4,500

The maximum regret is minimised by selecting P2.

10.18 The correct answer is: 2 and 3 only.

Statement 1 is false. As an average the expected value probably won't actually occur in any single event so it does not represent a probable outcome. It is more appropriate for repeated events (for example expected sales each year for many years). By the same logic statement 3 is true.

Statement 2 is true. Expected values fail to show the spread of possible values, therefore hiding the best/worst outcomes from the decision making process.

Statement 3 is true, the expected value is a **long-run average** and is unlikely to occur as a single outcome in the short-run.

Statement 4 is false. Risk is calculable (known or estimated probabilities and / or outcomes), uncertainty is not (either probabilities or some outcomes are unknown). In any event expected values show a long-run average outcome but they do not eliminate risk (or uncertainty).

10.19 The correct answer is: 2.6%.

Sales price affects sales revenue. A sensitivity calculation states how far in percentage terms contribution can fall before NPV (currently $1,300) reaches zero.

The present value of sales revenue is currently $50,025, so this could afford to drop by $1,300/$50,025, or 2.6%.

10.20 The correct answer is: Statement 2 - with simulation, more than one variable can change at a time.

Statement 1 - there is no decision rule with simulations – it is not an 'optimising' technique.

Statement 2 - this a clear advantage that simulations have over sensitivity analysis.

Statement 3 is incorrect. The input variables and distributions are estimates.

Statement 4 has some validity potentially, but is not necessarily the case. This advantage relates more to decision trees.

10.21 The correct answer is: $0.44.

Prob	No. of units sold	Variable costs	Cont per unit	Cont	Fixed costs	Profit / (loss)
	$	$	$	$	$	$
0.2×0.1=0.02	20,000	12	8	160,000	175,000	(15,000)
0.2×0.6 =0.12	20,000	14	6	120,000	175,000	(55,000)
0.2×0.3 =0.06	20,000	16	4	80,000	175,000	(95,000)
0.5×0.1 =0.05	30,000	12	8	240,000	175,000	65,000
0.5×0.6 =0.3	30,000	14	6	180,000	175,000	5,000
0.5×0.3 =0.15	30,000	16	4	120,000	175,000	(55,000)
0.3×0.1=0.03	40,000	12	8	320,000	175,000	145,000
0.3×0.6 =0.18	40,000	14	6	240,000	175,000	65,000
0.3×0.3 =0.09	40,000	16	4	160,000	175,000	(15,000)

Probability of making a loss = 0.02 + 0.12 + 0.06 + 0.15 + 0.09
= 0.44

10.22 The correct answer is: $1,000.

Prob	No sold '000	Var costs	Unit cont	Cont	Fixed costs	Profit / (loss)	Expt Value
0.3×0.2=0.06	20	12	8	160,000	175,000	(15,000)	(900)
0.3×0.5 =0.15	20	14	6	120,000	175,000	(55,000)	(8,250)
0.3×0.3 =0.09	20	16	4	80,000	175,000	(95,000)	(8,550)
0.4×0.2=0.08	30	12	8	240,000	175,000	65,000	5,200
0.4×0.5 =0.2	30	14	6	180,000	175,000	5,000	1,000
0.4×0.3 =0.12	30	16	4	120,000	175,000	(55,000)	(6,600)
0.3×0.2=0.06	40	12	8	320,000	175,000	145,000	8,700
0.3×0.5 =0.15	40	14	6	240,000	175,000	65,000	9,750
0.3×0.3 =0.09	40	16	4	160,000	175,000	(15,000)	(1,350)
							(1,000)

10.23 The correct answers are:

- The speed of processing is improved

- The cost of a computer system is lower than the manual system it replaces, mainly because the jobs previously performed by human operators are now done by computers

- The accuracy of data/information and processing is improved, because a computer does not make mistakes

Effectiveness on the other hand focuses primarily on the relationship of the organisation with its environment. An example is where automation is pursued because it is expected the company will be more effective at increasing market share or satisfying customer needs. Another example is where front office systems are developed to improve the organisation's decision-making capability to improve the effectiveness of the organisation.

10.24 The correct answers are:

- Information about personnel from the payroll system

- Value of sales from the accounting records; Information on decisions taken from the minutes of a meeting

- Information on decisions taken from the minutes of a meeting

Data and information captured from internal sources come from transaction systems, such as the payroll system and the receivables ledger, or is communicated formally or informally, as in a decision taken at a meeting.

Although the other two types of information mentioned are circulated within the organisation, they are both captured from outside. For example, the source of employment legislation is the government and the source of the market information is the market itself, which is clearly external to the organisation.

10.25 The correct answer is: Risk hedging is taking action to offset one risk by incurring a new risk in the opposite direction.

Some operational risks will be high frequency, high severity risks. The management of a portfolio of different risks is risk pooling or risk diversification. Insurance companies will insist that businesses take some action to reduce many risks as a condition of insuring those risks.

10.26 The correct answer is: 51%.

Sensitivity = NPV of a project / PV of the cashflow affected × 100%

NPV = $320,000 and PV of sales revenue = $630,000.

Sensitivity = $320,000 / $630,000 × 100% = 50.79% which is closest to 51%.

10.27 The correct answer is: 11%

Sensitivity = NPV of a project / PV of the cashflow affected × 100%

= 42,500 / 385,000 × 100% = 11.04% ≈ 11%

10.28 The correct answer is: A framework of fundamental principles.

CIMA's Code of Ethics is based on fundamental principles.

10.29 The correct answers are:

The value of perfect information is the difference between the EV of profit with perfect information and the EV of profit without perfect information.

The value of imperfect information is the difference between the EV of profit with imperfect information and the EV of profit without the information.

Practice mock questions

Questions

1   Strudel Co is a pet food manufacturer whose main production lines are dog food and cat food. In addition Strudel Co also produces food for birds and other small animals. An ABC system has recently been introduced to apportion set-up costs to Strudel Co's product lines.

In the latest period there were 800 production runs, 400 related to dog food and 200 to cat food. Total set-up costs were $180,000.

What set-up costs were charged to the cat food product line?

☐ $60,000
☐ $45,000
☐ $90,000
☐ $120,000

2   Costs are often classified into four categories:

i   Unit
ii   Batch
iii   Product
iv   Facility sustaining

When will ABC deliver most value as a device for costing a business's different products?

☐   If most costs consist of (i) and (iv).
☐   If most costs consist of (i) and (iii).
☐   If most costs consist of (ii) and (iii).
☐   If most costs consist of (iii) and (iv).

3   **Which of the following organisational characteristics make it LEAST likely that a JIT manufacturing approach would be beneficial?**

☐   Low inventory holding costs accounting for less than 5% of total costs.
☐   Poor industrial relations, strikes are common.
☐   Short production lead times.
☐   Seasonal demand, 75% of output is sold in the Christmas trading season.

4   V provides administrative and support services such as call centre work, payroll, invoicing and other documentation processing. Currently, V has 3 clients: Client A, Client E and Client S.

Client E

is a health service provider. V carries out routine administrative tasks on medical records for E.

Client A

is a manufacturer of electrical components. V undertakes invoicing payments for A.

Client S

is a bank. V provides a call centre service for S.

Other information:

Total overheads incurred in the year were $1,900 million.

The Finance Director has advised that overheads for Clients A and S should be apportioned according to the equivalent units of work activity completed. It is estimated that approximately 30% of total overheads can be attributed to Client E.

Client A:

32 million invoices have been processed.

Client S:

Calls handled: 80 million by an average of 4,000 direct employees. On average, each call dealt with for Client S takes approximately 20% more time to process than the average time spent processing an invoice Client A. Hence, the equivalent units of work activity should reflect the average extra time taken to deal with a call compared with processing accounting records for Client A.

What is the amount of overhead that Client S will be charged with?

- ☐ $997.5m
- ☐ $332.5m
- ☐ $1,423.5m
- ☐ $1,281m

---

5   **Where decommissioning costs are likely to be high, this is an argument for the use of:**

- ☐ Target costing
- ☐ Kaizen
- ☐ Lifecycle costing
- ☐ Value analysis

---

6   A management accountant in a public sector (ie government finance and not for profit) hospital is examining the viability of using Activity Based Management techniques.

Which of the following would influence the decision over whether or not to use ABC?

- ☐ Many different medical services being provided
- ☐ Overheads are high relative to direct costs
- ☐ Customers do not pay for their medical treatment
- ☐ Quality is the key concern of patients

---

7   The latest financial results (and forecasts) of C Ltd are disappointing. The Board of C Ltd have made the following observations:

Director D – poor logistics and quality combined with out of date designs have led to the loss of contracts with major clients.

Director T – product improvements are being held back by a conservative culture within the company.

Director P – staff have not received a pay rise in recent years and are obstructive and reluctant to participate in change programmes.

A TQM programme is being recommended by the CEO of Company C, who has suggested the importance of the following:

i   Involvement of everyone in the programme.

ii   Focus on continuous improvement.

iii   Emphasis on inter-departmental cooperation.

iv   Focus the TQM programme on meeting the needs of external customers.

What are the critical success factors in the implementation of a TQM programme for C Ltd?

☐   (i) and (iii)
☐   (ii) and (iii)
☐   (iii) and (iv)
☐   (i), (ii) and (iii)

---

8   **Which of the following is likely to result from the use of value analysis?**

Select all that apply.

☐   Better prices from suppliers due to a less diverse product range resulting in larger order sizes
☐   A reduction in costs and quality
☐   Use of more expensive parts leading to higher prices
☐   Higher sales volume
☐   Higher sales price

---

9   Supermarket X has re-designed its milk cartons so that they are sold in large plastic sachets. As a result the amount of non-recycled plastic being used by X has fallen by 22%.

The new approach required the following:

•   Making customers aware of how much non-recycled plastic was being used in the original product.

•   Setting targets for reduction in use of non-recycled plastic.

What are the above measures an example of?

☐   The experience curve effect
☐   Kaizen costing
☐   Value analysis
☐   TQM

---

10   Company Z is evaluating a proposal to produce a new type of bus, which will be powered by a radical new fuel cell that will reduce its emission of harmful greenhouse gasses to zero.

The target selling price is $100,000, and the target profit is $10,000 per vehicle.

As a result of a target costing analysis based on a prototype design, Z has identified a cost gap of $2,000 per vehicle.

Which of the following would be an appropriate response to this cost gap?

☐   Increase the selling price by $2,000 per vehicle.
☐   Abandon the proposal.
☐   Apply value engineering to attempt to reduce costs.
☐   Reduce the desired margin by $2,000 per vehicle.

---

11   **Which of the following statements is correct?**

☐   A 75% learning curve represents a faster rate of learning than a 70% learning curve because it measures the amount that the average time per unit will fall to each time cumulative production doubles.

☐   A 70% learning curve represents a faster rate of learning than a 75% learning curve because it measures the amount that the average time per unit will fall by each time cumulative production doubles.

☐   A 75% learning curve represents a faster rate of learning than a 70% learning curve because it measures the amount that the time per unit will fall by each time an extra unit is produced.

☐   A 70% learning curve represents a faster rate of learning than a 75% learning curve because it measures the amount that the average time per unit will fall to each time cumulative production doubles.

---

12   B Co is an aircraft manufacturer. One of B CO's main products is a small aircraft suitable for short-range passenger transport. This product was launched two years ago.

In the first year of production 100 aircraft were produced, and the average time taken for producing each aircraft was 22.7 hours.

Last year 200 aircraft were produced taking a total of 2,511 hours.

Over this period B Co has experienced a 80% learning curve effect – this is the norm in B Co's industry and is expected to continue.

The learning index for an 80% learning curve effect is -0.322.

B Co is planning to produce 400 aircraft in the coming year. How many hours should it budget to produce these aircraft?

☐   3,689
☐   5,389
☐   8,470
☐   2,511

13 Sudsy Co makes high quality cleaning products for use in hospitals.

A new product, the Sudsy Extreme, is produced in batches of 2,000. Sudsy Co anticipates a learning curve effect.

Data for the first 2 batches is given below.

Batch	Material cost	Labour cost
1	$1,000	$1,000
2	$1,000	$800

What will the total prime cost of the next 4,000 units be?

- ☐ $2,640
- ☐ $5,240
- ☐ $3,440
- ☐ $5,280

---

14 Bergson Co is an established manufacturer of durable stylish luggage for wealthy travellers.

In Bergson Co's experience, a learning curve effect of 90% occurs but only for the first 100 batches produced.

Bergson is planning the labour budget for next year for product X.

This product has been produced for the past 4 years, and 90 batches have been produced to date, taking a total time of 454 hours. The first batch took 10 hours to complete.

The learning index for a 90% learning curve effect is -0.152.

Next year Bergson is planning to make 30 batches.

How many labour hours should Bergson budget for this output? (to the nearest hour)

	labour hours

Work to three decimal places in all of your workings.

---

15 Cantor Co has started producing a new toy light sabre to coincide with the launch of a new film based on space travel.

The first four batches of light sabres took 100 hours, the next 12 took 80 hours.

What rate of learning is indicated by this data?

- ☐ 45.0%
- ☐ 67.1%
- ☐ 80.0%
- ☐ Not possible to assess with this data.

---

16 A company is able to sell different versions of the same core product to different market segments at different prices.

Which ONE of the following pricing strategies is being applied?

☐ Market skimming
☐ Price differentiation
☐ Price discrimination
☐ Premium pricing

17 **Which of the following statements are likely to be true?**

Select ALL that apply.

☐ Market skimming is more common where a product is expected to have a shorter product life cycle.

☐ Market penetration is especially suitable where a significant experience curve effect exists.

☐ Product bundling can be used to maximise revenues where demand is elastic.

☐ Losses in the early stages of the product life cycle are due to a loss leadership strategy being followed.

18 **Which of the following statements is likely to be true?**

☐ In a perfectly competitive market, a price skimming strategy will only be appropriate at the early stages of the product life cycle.

☐ Loss leadership strategy is likely to be a short-term strategy.

☐ High price elasticity implies that a company has greater flexibility over price setting.

☐ Product bundling can be used to create higher revenue than would be obtained by selling products separately.

19 Barium Co sells health food snacks called Nibbles. Each pack currently sells for $1.50, and demand is currently 120,000 packs per month. Based on a trial of higher prices in a test market, Barium Co estimates that demand would fall by 5,000 for every $0.10 increase in the price of a pack.

The contribution per unit is $0.30 per pack.

Calculate the optimal selling price of a pack of Nibbles, to two decimal places.

$ [   ]

20 Steiner Co is a manufacturer of high quality hand-made guitars, and other musical instruments.

Currently Steiner Co charges $1,000 per guitar and sells 260 per year. It is estimated that Steiner Co could sell 300 per year if it cut prices to $800.

What is the maximum revenue to the nearest $ that Steiner Co can achieve?

$ [   ]

21 **Which ONE of the following conditions are likely to fit well with a market-penetration pricing strategy?**

☐ A firm has high levels of liquidity
☐ The product life cycle is short
☐ The product is unique and has no direct competitors
☐ Intense competition with a small number of large well-resourced rivals

22   Division G is a division of Axio Co, and has been set up as an investment centre. Axio is a conglomerate that supports its business units with an active Finance Department that deals with cash management and credit control for the group as a whole. Other matters are under divisional control, although often require Head Office approval.

Axio intends to evaluate Division G on the basis of its ROCE.

Which TWO of the following should be included in the calculation of Division G's ROCE?

- ☐   Interest payments on Division G's borrowings
- ☐   Division G's cash holdings
- ☐   Division G's receivables
- ☐   Apportioned overheads from Axio Co analysed using ABC
- ☐   Division G's non-current assets

---

23   Sparkle is a division of Crystal Co. The latest information for Sparkle is shown below together with further detail on Sparkle's profits:

Asset base $15m

Profits before tax $1.2m

- •   Depreciation on Sparkle's controllable asset base was $0.3m.
- •   Apportioned head office expenses were $0.2m.
- •   Finance costs were $0.1m.

Crystal Co expects a return of 10% on the assets of this division.

Calculate the controllable residual income (RI) of Sparkle in $m, to the nearest million.

$m   [   ]

---

24   **Which of the following ratios would be used to measure an organisation's financial risk as part of the financial aspect of the balanced scorecard?**

Select ALL that apply.

- ☐   Interest cover
- ☐   Asset turnover
- ☐   Gearing
- ☐   Profit margin

---

25   **Which of the following is not an advantage of using non financial performance measures (NFPIs) over financial performance measures (FPMs)?**

- ☐   NFPIs are easier to manipulate
- ☐   FPMs are backward looking
- ☐   NFPIs are easier to understand
- ☐   NFPIs provide less of a short-term focus
- ☐   FPMs are not available as quickly as NFPIs

26 An airline is considering the design of its balanced scorecard.

To which quadrant of the balanced scorecard would a measure of production lead times relate?

☐ Innovation and growth
☐ Customer satisfaction
☐ Financial success
☐ Internal business processes

---

27 Division W is currently making operating profits of $3m on an asset base of $18m. It is considering the following two investments:

	Project A	Project B
Investment	$2m	$3m
Forecast annual operating profit	$0.26m	$0.54m

Division W has been set a target ROCE of 12% by its Head Office.

Which of the following investments decisions would be taken by Division W, based on the above information?

☐ Invest in project A
☐ Invest in project B
☐ Invest in neither project
☐ Invest in both projects

---

28 EVA, RI, ROI and the balanced scorecard are all important performance measures. The following criticisms each relate to one of these.

Match the criticism with the one performance measure listed above that it is most relevant to:

Difficult to use to compare divisions.

Likely to lead to sub-optimal decision-making.

May lead to information overload.

Hard to use because of the complications in calculations.

---

29 M&M Co have recently introduced a new corporate social responsibility program. This committed the company to choosing more environmentally friendly forms of corporate travel for their employees. This would be achieved by controlling the number of miles travelled, by encouraging more environmentally friendly forms of travel and by encouraging the use of video conferencing.

M&M is committed to demonstrating success in these areas over a 3 year period.

Data for M&M over the past 3 years is given below:

	20X1	20X2	20X3
No. employees	4,000	3,500	3,000
No. video conferences	100	120	150
No. miles travelled	200,000	175,000	150,000
CO2 emissions	1,500	1,400	1,200

Which TWO of the following statements about M&M are likely to be true, based on the above data?

☐ CO2 emissions have been effectively controlled by the introduction of new policies.
☐ Video conferencing has consistently grown in popularity.
☐ The number of miles travelled by employees has fallen.
☐ Video conferencing has caused a fall in the number of miles travelled.

---

30   L Co is a DIY retailer. A summary of L Co's latest financial results are as follows:

	$m
Sales	225
Operating profit	50
Profit before tax	40
Profit after tax	30
Non current assets	150
Net current assets	50
Long-term liabilities	100
Equity	100

Which of the following is a correct summary of L Co's performance?

- ☐   Asset turnover 1.5   Operating margin 22.2%
- ☐   Asset turnover 2.0   Operating margin 17.8%
- ☐   Asset turnover 1.125   Operating margin 22.2%
- ☐   Asset turnover 2.25   Operating margin 22.2%

---

31   D Co is an under-performing parcel delivery company.

It has been suggested to D Co should use benchmarking to attempt to achieve a radical breakthrough in performance that is required to ensure corporate survival.

Which ONE of the following types of benchmarking is most likely to be appropriate for D Co?

- ☐   Competitive benchmarking.

- ☐   Joining an industry database to analyse performance against KPIs for the parcel delivery industry.

- ☐   Internal benchmarking.

- ☐   Benchmarking against a company outside the parcel delivery sector with a reputation for excellent logistics.

---

32   At a recent Board meeting to discuss the implementation of the Balanced Scorecard the following statements were made.

Which of these statements is true?

- ☐   There must be a maximum of two performance measures in each part of the balanced scorecard to avoid information overload.

- ☐   The measures in the scorecard must be given a weighting – with the financial measures being given the highest weighting.

- ☐   Care must be taken to ensure that the innovation and learning measures complement the key internal business and customer measures.

- ☐   There must be a minimum of two performance measures in each part of the balanced scorecard to ensure that enough KPIs are being given visibility at corporate level.

33   Division Y is currently making operating profits of $6.5m on an asset base of $130m.

It is considering the following investment:

Project 315

Investment	$25m
Forecast annual operating profit	$1.7m

Division W has been set a target return of 8% by its Head Office.

How would the use of ROI or RI motivate the senior managers at Division Y to operate in the best interest of the company as a whole?

☐   ROI (only) would incorrectly reject project 315.
☐   RI (only) would incorrectly reject project 315.
☐   Neither ROI or RI would incorrectly reject project 315.
☐   Both ROI and RI would incorrectly reject project 315.

---

34   Poggeral Co makes coffee beans which are sold internally to is coffee shop division, and also to up-market food retailers. When Poggeral Co sells to these retailers it incurs packaging costs of $2 per kg of coffee beans. At present Poggeral Co is operating at full capacity.

The external market price available to Poggeral Co is $20 / kg, and at this price Poggeral Co achieves a contribution / sales ratio of 30%.

Poggeral has sufficient capacity to sell to both the internal and the external market.

At what price per kg should the coffee beans be sold to the coffee shop division?

Give your answer to the nearest $.

$ ☐

---

35   Division Z has high levels of surplus capacity and as a result has agree to manufacture a significant order for Division T at a transfer price equal to its variable cost.

The Head Office of the company that Division Z is a part of has decided that it is unfair that Division Z has not made a profit on this transaction and has decided that a change should be made to the agreed transfer price. Head Office have made it clear that this is not a matter for debate, saying that *"it is clearly fair that division Z makes a fair share of the profit, and we will not allow any further time to be spent on this issue. We all have far better things to spending time on"*.

Which TWO of the following courses of action will be likely to be appropriate here?

☐   A dual tariff transfer pricing system could be introduced.
☐   A two-part tariff system could be introduced.
☐   A full cost + basis could be used as the transfer price.
☐   An opportunity cost basis could be used.

36   Division X makes windscreen wipers which are sold internally other divisions who use them in the manufacture of various types of vehicles.

Division X also sells these externally for $10 / unit but incurs selling costs of $2 and ultimately makes contribution of $3 / unit.

Division X is currently operating with high levels of surplus capacity.

The current transfer price for internally sold units is $5 /unit but this has caused considerable debate at Division X.

Which ONE of the following is true?

☐   The current transfer price is too low because it will fail to motivate Division X to make units for internal sale.

☐   The current transfer price is too low because it will encourage external sales and deprive internal divisions of this component forcing them to buy externally for $10/unit.

☐   The current transfer price recognizes the true cost of the internally transferred units and therefore should not be changed.

☐   A transfer price of $9 would be better as an estimate of the true cost of the internally transferred units.

---

37   A consumer electronics firm, Moover Co, currently makes all of its products from its home country, which is in Europe.

Moover Co is assessing a proposal to build a new factory in Asia and to transfer some of the operations from Europe to Asia, to reduce its operating costs.

Which TWO of the following are relevant cash flows that should be included in the appraisal of this project?

☐   Sales revenue from the products being sold by the Asian factory.
☐   Redundancy costs for European workers that are affected by this investment.
☐   A cut in dividends that would be needed to free up cash for the project.
☐   Opportunity cost of lost sales due to disruption to production caused by the investment.
☐   Interest costs on a loan that would be taken out to build the Asian factory.

---

38   West College is a college based in Region X.

In order to expand its student intake it is exploring the possibility of opening up a new campus in Region Y.

If student numbers are poor after the first year the venture will be abandoned.

However, because students will have booked on a 2 year course the venture cannot be fully closed until the end of year 2.

West College estimates the chance of abandonment to be 25%.

The facilities management department have identified two suitable sites.

Site A will require refurbishment costs of $100,000 and will cost $300,000 per year to lease. The term of the lease is 4 years.

Site B will be leased fully furnished and will also cost $300,000 per year to lease. The term of the lease is also 4 years, but there is a break clause at the end of year 2 which allows West College to cancel the lease at that point with no further penalty. This site will require an additional up-front payment which is currently being negotiated.

West College's cost of capital is 10%.

BPP
LEARNING MEDIA

Which of the following is the maximum acceptable additional up-front payment that West College should make in order to secure Site B instead of Site A?

☐ $530,200
☐ $207,550
☐ $430,200
☐ $107,550

39   Spice Co is a dynamic and fashionable manufacturer of IT and communications devices. Recently it has launched a new virtual reality headset, the NL.

This has not had the success that Spice Co had hoped for.

Technological problems with the NL meant that Spice Co spent twice as much on start-up costs. Sales have also been sluggish and as a result Spice Co has not been able to sell at as high a price as it had originally planned.

Currently the NT is making significant losses, although it is making a positive contribution.

Spice Co is considering whether or not to stop production of the NT.

Which TWO of the following are valid factors to consider in this decision?

☐ The overspend on NT's set-up costs.
☐ The losses being made by NT.
☐ The impact on Spice Co's brand name of exiting from this market.
☐ The price that the NT is currently being sold for.
☐ The future prospects for NT sales.

40   Poison Co is planning a new investment. The cost will be $1,200,000 and the investment will attract tax allowable depreciation at a rate of 20% on a reducing balance basis. The investment will be made in the final week of the current financial year.

The project has an expected life of 10 years and an expected residual value of $100,000.

The company pays tax at a rate of 25%, and tax is paid one year after the end of the year in which the profit was earned.

Poison Co has a cost of capital of 10%.

Calculate the present value of tax saved in year 2 from tax allowable depreciation, giving your answer to the nearest $.

$ ☐

41   A finance manager chooses to evaluate an investment project using IRR rather than NPV.

Which TWO of the following explanations would justify her decision?

☐   Low interest rates mean that there is less emphasis placed on the time value of money.

☐   Managers understand IRR better than NPV.

☐   An absolute measure is required, to measure the extent to which competing project create shareholder wealth.

☐   There is uncertainty over the appropriate cost of capital to use.

42   A project has an initial investment of $225,000 and is expected deliver an IRR of 12% over a four year period.

Assuming that the cash flows are received equally every year, what are the annual cash inflows from the project? Give your answer to the nearest $.

$ [   ]

43   Two alternative types of new aircraft are being evaluated for use by new airline, Drucken Co.

The key details are as follows:

Type A   NPV $32,000   IRR   22%
Type B   NPV $22,000   IRR   30%

The NPV has been calculated at Drucken Co's cost of capital of 10%.

Which ONE of the following statements will be true?

☐   At a cost of capital of higher than 22%, type B will be chosen.
☐   Type A will be chosen, assuming the financial analysis has been performed correctly.
☐   In the absence of capital rationing constraints, both type A and type B should be fully financed.
☐   IRR is not appropriate for this decision because it ignores the time value of money.

44   Sid Co is evaluating an investment using NPV.

During the analysis it has been noted that there is only one rate of inflation (3%) that affects sales revenue and operating costs in the same way.

The rate of tax is 25%, and Sid Co will benefit from tax savings due to capital allowance that result from the capital investment.

Sid Co is all equity financed and its shareholders expect a return of 10%.

Which ONE of the following statements is true?

☐   It will be simpler and equally accurate to discount the real cash flows at 10%.

☐   The cost of capital will have to be adjusted to 6.8% before being used to discount the money cash flows.

☐   The cost of capital will have to be adjusted to 6.8% before being used to discount the real flows.

☐   It will be more accurate to discount the money cash flows using the 10% cost of capital.

45   Carmelita Co is a company that in the past has specialized in training medical professionals. It is now planning a diversification into drama schools.

Carmelita Co has projected the following operating profits based on a start of cost of $100,000 which will be fully written off during the 5 year life of the project, starting from year 2 when the school will open.

Year	1	2	3	4	5
Forecast profit ($'000s)		20	40	45	60

Calculate the payback period for this project. Give your answer in years, to one decimal place.

[   ]

46 VFD Co is a small company that is experiencing cash flow pressures. VFD Co have just had an animated Board meeting at which the topic of project appraisal was discussed.

Which TWO of the following statements are likely to be true for VFD?

☐ Payback should be emphasised much more strongly given VFD's circumstances.

☐ VFD should change its simple payback period target of 2 years to a discounted (adjusted) payback period of 2 years.

☐ Project investment should be suspended during periods of cash shortages.

☐ VFD needs to focus on short-term profitability, so it should primarily use ARR as its main project appraisal technique.

---

47 F Co is evaluating a two year project which will provide a return of $0.75m per year on an investment of $1.2m.

The project has been correctly analysed as follows:

- NPV at 10% $101,250
- NPV at 17% ($10,673)

F Co's cost of capital is 10%.

Using this data, assess which one of the following is the correct estimate for F Co's modified IRR.

☐ 19.8%
☐ 18.3%
☐ 14.6%
☐ 16.5%

---

48 Pavlova Co runs a chain of up-market confectionary stores.

Currently Pavlova Co has a cash surplus of $1,000,000 which is planning to return to shareholders.

However an opportunity has come up to buy a new store for $1 million.

Pavlova Co has decided to obtain the new store, but is unsure whether to rent it or buy it.

Pavlova Co has a cost of capital of 8% and evaluates projects over a 5 year period.

In 5 years' time the disposal value of the Store will have depreciated by 40% from the price paid by Pavlova Co.

Rent payments would be made at the end of each year.

What is the maximum rent per year that Pavlova Co would be willing to pay (ignore tax)? Give your answer to the nearest $.

$ _____

49 A project has the following characteristics:

- It has an initial cash outflow followed by a series of positive cash flows.
- The NPV is positive at a cost of capital of 10%.
- The IRR is 20%.

In this situation which TWO of the following statements are true?

☐ The MIRR will be lower than the IRR.
☐ The MIRR will be above the IRR.
☐ The MIRR may be below the cost of capital.
☐ The MIRR will be above the cost of capital.

---

50 A company has $200,000 to invest in new projects this year.

All investments must be started now and all projects are indivisible.

There are four investment opportunities – these are outlined below.

Project	Initial investment ($'000s)	NPV	PI ($'000s)
1	100	40	0.36
2	120	63	0.54
3	70	36	0.51
4	20	20	1

What is the NPV of the optimal project selection to the nearest $'000?

☐ 114
☐ 99
☐ 143
☐ 159

---

51 Conrad Co has a number of projects that it would like to invest in this year. All of the projects are divisible and are projected to deliver a positive NPV. All of the projects will deliver cash inflows from next year onwards.

However, Conrad Co is facing a soft capital rationing problem and is unable to finance all of these projects.

In this situation, which TWO of the following courses of action may be appropriate?

☐ Rank the projects using MIRR.
☐ Rank the projects using NPV.
☐ Use external sources of finance eg borrowing.
☐ Rank the projects using the profitability index.

52 Ent Co is a car rental company. Ent Co's customers expect to rent new cars that are in excellent condition, so Ent Co has in the past bought new cars and kept them for a year and then has sold them.

The typical costs of this are as follows:

Time	0	1
Purchase	($25,000)	
Running cost		($2,000)
Disposal proceeds		$11,000
Net cash flows	($25,000)	$9,000
Discount @ 10%	1	0.909
Present value	($25,000)	$8,181
Total present value	($16,819)	

Ent Co is now considering moving to a 2 year replacement cycle.

The estimated net cost (taking into account disposal value and running costs) is $6,500 in year 2.

What is the equivalent annual cost of the optimal replacement cycle?

- ☐ $18,503 for a 1 year replacement cycle.
- ☐ $18,541 for a 2 year replacement cycle.
- ☐ Not relevant because the negative NPV indicates that it is not worth leasing the vehicles.
- ☐ $12,743 for a 1 year replacement cycle.

---

53 BC Co has bought a licence to drill for oil in the North Sea. In recent years oil prices have fallen and this oil field is not worth developing at the moment. However, if the oil price changes in the future or production costs fall due to advances in technology, then this oil field may become profitable. It is expected that the oil field will also contain significant reserves of natural gas.

BC Co there has an option to wait as a result of this licence.

Which of the following factors would increase the value of this option to wait?

Select ALL that apply.

- ☐ An increase in the volatility of the oil price
- ☐ A longer licence period
- ☐ Tighter regulations over the award of licenses to drill
- ☐ A rise in the demand for natural gas

---

54 Café Salo orders fresh pastries every day for $10 / batch and then sells them in store for $25. At the end of each day any unsold pastries are given to staff or thrown away.

The café has estimated the following demand:

Daily demand (batches)	Probability
20	0.25
40	0.3
60	0.45

Café Salo is experiencing liquidity problems and wishes to choose the order quantity with the best 'worst-case' outcome.

What profit per day will Café Salo make if it selects the appropriate order quantity? Give your answer to the nearest $.

$ [   ]

55   The following is a list of techniques that can be used to evaluate projects:

- Discounted payback period
- Expected values
- Simulation
- Sensitivity analysis

Match the criticisms below to the technique above that they are most relevant to.

Based on subjective probabilities.

Ignores the importance of later cash flows.

Only considers the impact of changing one variable at a time.

Complex and time-consuming.

---

56   The risk of a project is being analysed by a company using sensitivity analysis.

The project is for 4 years and is expected to generated annual revenues of $420,000, annual variable costs of $160,000, and annual fixed costs of $50,000.

The initial investment will be $650,000 and the cost of capital is 10%.

The project NPV has been correctly calculated as $15,700.

Calculate the sensitivity of this project to the assumed level of sales volume, as a percentage to 1 decimal place.

---

57   An oil exploration company, S Co, is reviewing the results of a preliminary analysis of three oil fields that it is considering investing in.

The W field is based on land and is estimated to contain mainly oil with a small amount of natural gas.

The X field is also based on land (in country B) and would require a controversial techniques known as fracking to access the oil and gas reserves.

The Y field is based at sea, in shallow water, and is estimated to contain equal amounts of gas and the Z field is based at sea, in deep water, and is estimated to contain equal amounts of gas and oil.

The estimated profits from these three proposed investments have been evaluated using three possible scenarios – which are based on three possible scenarios concerning the oil price, the price of gas, the pace of technological change and the likelihood of gaining public approval for fracking in country B.

Scenario	W field	X field	Y field	Z field
1	$90m	$100m	$20m	$60m
2	$70m	$80m	$40m	$50m
3	$65m	$60m	$90m	$40m

S Co intends choose the field that leads to the lowest maximum regret.

Which field will S Co select?

- ☐ Field W
- ☐ Field X
- ☐ Field Y
- ☐ Field Z

58   P Co is a house-builder. It has been offered the possibility of buying land and then applying for planning permission to build a new housing estate.

If the planning application is successful then the profit from building the housing estate is predicted to be $120m or $80m (before considering the cost of the land) depending on the amount of lower value social housing that P Co is required to build. There is an equal chance of either outcome.

There is also a small chance (estimated as having a 20% probability) that planning permission will be refused in which case the land will be worth 5% of the expected gain from this investment.

The current land owner is asking for $40m for the land.

What would P Co's expected profits be if it proceeded with this investment? Give your answer in $m to 1 decimal place.

$m [   ]

---

59   Z Co is a European retailer. Most of its clothes are made in Asia and then transported to its single warehouse in Spain.

A risk assessment has identified this warehouse as a key area of risk. If there was any disruption to the operation of this warehouse then there would be a major impact on Z Co's ability to trade.

To date there have been no problems but if any did occur (eg earthquake, strike action) then there would be serious problems for Z Co.

Which TWO of the following courses of action would be the most appropriate response to handling this type of risk?

☐   Business continuity insurance.

☐   Careful review of the performance of the warehouse to ensure its reliability.

☐   Take no action because there is risk inherent in any business, and this appears to be acceptable because there have been no problems to date.

☐   Diversify by building another smaller warehouse in another part of Europe.

---

60   Fearless Co is a retailer of film memorabilia such as posters, watches, wallets etc.

Fearless has been approached by Wermer Co, a large film studio, which has offered Fearless exclusive rights to sell a range of t-shirts related to the planned launch of a new 'blockbuster' film planned for the next summer holidays. Fearless would be expected to promote the range of t-shirts at an expected cost of $100,000.

It is in the nature of the industry that the products have a short shelf-life and any unsold stock would be disposed of at a fraction of the cost of producing them.

Fearless estimate that they could sell the t-shirts for an average price of $10 during the summer period when the film is launched, but would have to sell unsold stock for a price of $1 / unit.

The t-shirts would be supplied at a cost of $6 / unit.

Fearless estimates sales demand and payoffs (in $000s) as follows:

Order size		50,000	300,000	1,000,000	10,000,000
Demand	Probability				
50,000	0.1	100	-1,150	-4,650	-49,650
300,000	0.4	100	1,100	-2,400	-47,400
1,000,000	0.3	100	1,100	3,900	-41,100
10,000,000	0.2	100	1,100	3,900	39,900

Which order size should Fearless choose in order to maximise its expected profit?

☐　　50,000

☐　　300,000

☐　　1,000,000

☐　　10,000,000

Practice mock answers

Answers

1   The correct answer is: 45,000.

$180,000 / 800 production runs = $225 per run

$$\$225 \times 200 = \$45,000$$

It is easy to misread this question and to assume that there were 600 production runs (400 dog food and 200 cat food) but the question says that these are the MAIN products not the only products, and clearly states the total production runs as 800.

---

2   The correct answer is: If most costs consist of (ii) and (iii).

Unit related costs are typically direct costs and as such can be identified without using ABC.

It is very difficult to find accurate or meaningful cost drivers for facility sustaining costs (eg security / corporate advertising).

However, if overhead costs can be tracked to batches or products then this can provided insight in terms of differing product costs.

---

3   The correct answer is: Seasonal demand, 75% of output is sold in the Christmas trading season.

This will make it very unlikely that zero inventory can be held in the run up to the Christmas season. It is hard for a business to change the pattern of sales demand so this is the scenario where JIT is least likely to be beneficial.

Notes on incorrect answers:

•	Low inventory holding costs accounting for less than 5% of total costs.	This makes JIT less attractive but saving on inventory costs is only one of the benefits of JIT. Other benefits (improved quality / quicker lead times) could still make JIT attractive.
•	Poor industrial relations, strikes are common.	This makes JIT harder to use because stock-outs will occur during strike action. However, it could be argued that a zero inventory philosophy will force a company to deal with its industrial relations problems and this could be beneficial.
•	Short production lead times.	This makes JIT more practical because it is more practical to wait for customer orders before commencing production.

---

4   The correct answer is: $997.5m.

Total overheads	$1,900m
Client E (30% × $1,900m)	$570m
Balance to apportion	$1,330m
Equivalent units	
Client A	32m
Client S (80m × 1.2)	96m
Total equivalent units	128m
Apportionment	
Client A: $1,330m × 32 / 128	$332.5m
Client S: $1,330m × 96 / 128	$997.5m

---

5   The correct answer is: Lifecycle costing

Lifecycle costing is based on analysing the costs over the whole lifecycle including decommissioning – it can be used to evaluate whether a product launch is viable if decommissioning costs are high.

---

6   The correct answer is: Many different medical services being provided

ABC is useful in understanding the true cost of providing different services.

Notes on incorrect answers:

- Overheads are low relative to direct costs.

   ABC is useful for understanding costs where overheads are high, and are therefore a key cost category.

- Customers do not pay for their medical treatment.

   Central government will be funding the hospital and will be concerned about cost control, so this does not impact on the decision to use ABC.

- Quality is the key concern of patients.

   Again central government will be funding the hospital and will be concerned about cost control, so this does not impact on the decision to use ABC.

---

7   The correct answer is: (i), (ii) and (iii).

- Involvement of everyone in the programme.
- Focus on continuous improvement.
- Emphasis on inter-departmental cooperation.

It is not only the final customer that matters in TQM – the intermediate customer matters too (eg work done for other 'internal' customers).

---

8   The correct answer is:

- Higher sales volume
- Higher sales price
- Better prices from suppliers due to a less diverse product range resulting in larger order sizes

Value analysis aims to raise value or reduce cost with no reduction in quality. As such it may result in higher sales volume or higher prices.

Redesign of a product to use a higher proportion of common parts can lead to better prices from suppliers due to a less diverse product range resulting in larger order sizes

Notes on incorrect answers:

- A reduction in costs and quality

   – Value analysis does not accept compromises in quality.

- Use of more expensive parts leading to higher prices

   – It is the value added by the parts that is the issue. Value analysis does not seek out higher cost parts unless they are absolutely essential.

9   The correct answer is: Value analysis.

Value analysis identifies non value added materials and implements appropriate change.

Kaizen is a process of continuous improvement that is centered on employee involvement.

The experience effect relates to the benefits of increased experience in producing a given product, and this is not the case here as the product is changing.

TQM aims to eliminate defects and this is not the issue here.

10   The correct answer is: Apply value engineering to attempt to reduce costs.

Notes on incorrect answers:

- Increase the selling price by $2,000 per vehicle.

  - The selling price is the starting point for target costing and will be the result of careful analysis of the appropriate positioning of the product. Adjusting the cost is the only acceptable way forward here.

- Abandon the proposal.

  - This would be potentially acceptable as an answer except that Z is looking at a prototype and therefore is at any early stage of the product evaluation, so abandoning at this stage would not be appropriate.

- Reduce the desired margin by $2,000 per vehicle.

  - This margin will have been chosen to deliver an acceptable return to investors, in line with the risk of the project, so by reducing the margin the project will no longer be generating an acceptable return. This is not acceptable.

11   The correct answer is: A 70% learning curve represents a faster rate of learning than a 75% learning curve because it measures the amount that the average time per unit will fall to each time cumulative production doubles.

This is because the learning curve measures the amount that the average time per unit will fall to each time cumulative production doubles, then the lower the percentage the greater the rate of learning.

12   The correct answer is: 3,689.

Using $y = ax^b$

The data from year 1 allows 'a' to be identified

$22.7 = a \times 100^{-0.322}$
$22.7 = a \times 0.227$
$a = 22.7 / 0.227 = 100$

This can then be applied to work out the average time for the overall output of 100 + 200 + 400 = 700.

So $y = 100 \times 0.121 = 12.1$ hours
So total time for 700 aircraft = 8,470.
Total taken in year 1 = 22.7 × 100 = 2,270
Total time taken in year 2 = 2,511
So total time for the forecast production of 400 aircraft = 8,470 − 2,270 − 2,511 = 3,689 hours.

13   The correct answer is: $3,440.

4,000 units = 2 more batches.

The average labour cost for the first 2 batches is (1,000 + 800) / 2 = $900.

Average labour cost has therefore fallen to 90% of its previous value as output has doubled.

So there is a 90% learning curve.

As output doubles from 2 to 4 average labour cost will fall again to 90% of its previous average ie 900 × 0.9 = $810.

So total labour cost = 4 × 810 = $3,240.

So the total labour cost for the 3rd and 4th batches = 3,240 − 800 − 1,000 = $1,440.

Assuming that material costs = $1,000 × 2 batches = $2,000 then total prime cost for the 3rd and 4th batches = $1,440 + $2,000 = $3,440.

---

14   The correct answer is: 126.

The learning effect will only occur for the next 10 batches.

This will raise cumulative output to 90 + 10 = 100.

So using $y = ax^b$
$y = 10 × 100^{-0.152}$ = 4.966 hours (to three decimal places).
Total time for 100 batches = 496.600 hours.
So the total time for the next 10 batches = 496.6 − 454 = 42.6 hours.

The remaining 20 batches will take the same time as the 100th batch.

The time taken for the 100th batch can be estimated by comparing the total time for 100 batches (496.6 hours as above) to the time taken for 99 batches.

So using $y =$
$y = 10$ = 4.974 hours.
Total time for 99 batches = 492.426 hours.
So total time for the 100th batch = 496.6 − 492.426 = 4.174 hours.
So the next 20 batches take 4.174 × 20 = 83.480 hours.
So total time for 30 batches = 42.6 + 83.48 = 126 hours (to the nearest hour).

Note: the solution allows a small amount of flexibility to allow for rounding issues.

---

15   The correct answer is: 67.1%.

Average time for 4 batches = 100 / 4 = 25.

Average time for a total of 16 batches = (100 + 80) / 16 = 11.25.

Moving from 4 to 16 batches represents output doubling twice (ie 4 batches × 2 = 8 batches, 8 × 2 = 16 batches).

So 25 × learning rate × learning rate = 11.25.
So 11.25 / 25 = 0.45 = learning effect × learning effect.
$\sqrt{0.45}$ = learning rate = 0.671 or 67.1%.

---

16   The correct answer is: Price differentiation.

Market skimming is a premium pricing strategy – this is not necessarily implied by the wording of the question.

Price discrimination involves selling the SAME product to different market segments at different prices.

---

17   The correct answers are:

- Market skimming is more common where a product is expected to have a shorter product life cycle.

- Market penetration is especially suitable where a significant experience curve effect exists.

Market skimming is more common where a product is expected to have a shorter product life cycle because there is a need to recoup the products costs via a high price during the product's short life.

Market penetration is especially suitable where a significant experience curve effect exists because an experience curve suggest that the quicker output rises the lower costs per unit will be. Low (penetration) pricing helps to stimulate higher demand and therefore higher output.

Notes on incorrect answers:

- Product bundling can be used to maximise revenues where demand is elastic.

    - Elastic demand (% change in demand / % change in price) means that consumers are sensitive to price rises. Bundling products together and selling at a higher price is unlikely to increase revenues in this case.

- Losses in the early stages of the product life cycle are due to a loss leadership strategy being followed.

    - It is possible / probable that products may not make profits in the early stages of the product life cycle but this does not necessarily imply that a loss leadership strategy is being used.

---

18   The correct answer is:

Product bundling can be used to create higher revenue than would be obtained by selling products separately.

Notes on incorrect answers:

- In a perfectly competitive market, a price skimming strategy will only be appropriate at the early stages of the product life cycle.

    - In a perfectly competitive market it will not be possible to charge a premium price at any stage of the life cycle.

- Loss leadership strategy is likely to be a short-term strategy.

    - No, it is often a long-term strategy to encourage consumers to buy related products (eg low prices for computer game consoles).

- High price elasticity implies that a company has greater flexibility over price setting.

    - High price elasticity (% change in demand / % change in price) means that consumers are very sensitive to price changes. This may be because of the availability of similar products from other firms. In this case it is harder to change prices.

19   Correct answer: $2.55.

Marginal revenue = a – 2bx

'a' is the price level at which demand falls to zero

Demand is currently 120,000 and would fall by 5,000 for every $0.10 price rise – so demand falls to zero when it has fallen by 120,000 and this would require 120,000 / 5,000 = 24 price rises of $0.10 ie a $2.40 price rise from its current level of $1.50 to $3.90.

'a' is $3.90
b = change in price / the change in quantity = 0.1/ 5,000 = 0.00002
so marginal revenue = 3.90 – 0.00004x

Profit is maximized where marginal revenue = marginal cost

If the contribution per pack is $0.30 per pack then the marginal cost is selling price – contribution = $1.50 – $0.30 = $1.20.

So marginal revenue = marginal cost where:

3.90 – 0.00004x = 1.20
So 3.90 – 1.20 = 0.00004x So 2.70 = 0.00004x
So 2.70 / 0.00004 = 67,500 units

The price that is needed to achieve this can be calculated using

P = a – bx
So P = 3.90 – 0.00002 (67,500) = $2.55

---

20   Correct answer: $264,500.

Marginal revenue = a – 2bx
'a' is the price level at which demand falls to zero

Demand is currently 260 and would change by 40 for every $200 price change – so demand falls to zero when it has fallen by 260 and this would require 260 / 40 = 6.5 prices rise of $200 ie a $1,300 price rise from its current level of $1,000 to $2,300.

'a' is $2,300
b = change in price / the change in quantity = 200 / 40 = 5
so marginal revenue = 2,300 – 10x

Revenue is maximized where no further revenue can be raised from price cuts ie MR = 0

So 2,300 – 10x = 0 So 2,300 = 10x
So 2,300 / 10 = 230 units
P = a – bx
So P = 2,300 – 5 (230) = $1,150

And at this price revenue will be price × quantity = $1,150 × 230 = $264,500

---

21 The correct answer is: A firm has high levels of liquidity.

This strategy is likely to require high set up costs in order to build capacity, therefore high levels of liquidity are helpful.

Notes on incorrect answers:

- The product life cycle is short

    - This is more commonly associated with a price skimming strategy.

- The product is unique and has no direct competitors

    - This is more commonly associated with a price skimming strategy.

- Intense competition with a small number of large well-resourced rivals

    - This makes a price war likely if a penetration pricing strategy is followed.

22 The correct answer is:

- Division G's non-current assets.
- Apportioned overheads from Axio Co analysed using ABC.

These are areas for which Division G can be held responsible because they are at least partly under its control (the use of ABC implies that the cost drivers used to apportion overheads are under the control of Division G).

Notes on incorrect answers:

- Interest payments on Division G's borrowings.

    - ROCE is calculated using profits before interest.

- Division G's cash holdings and receivables.

    - These areas are controlled by Head Office in this particular case.

23 The correct answer is: 0.

RI = controllable divisional profit before interest and tax − (required return × controllable asset base).

Here the controllable divisional PBIT = $1.2m + $0.2m (HO expenses are assumed to be uncontrollable) + $0.1m (interest) = $1.5m.

Required return = 0.1.

Controllable asset base is assumed to be $15m. So RI = 1.5 − (0.1 × 15) = 0.

24 The correct answers are:

- Interest cover
- Gearing

Both of these ratios measure the exposure of a firm to its debt liabilities ie financial risk. Asset turnover examines the efficiency with which assets are being used and profit margin measures return, not risk.

25   The correct answer is: NFPIs are easier to manipulate

FPMs are typically made available to management on a monthly or quarterly basis whereas NFPIs are typically available instantly (eg defects per shift, customer complaints per day). FPMs mainly focus on the past and the short-term, but if a company is achieving good performance in its key NFPIs then this is likely to indicate FUTURE success.

It is debatable whether NFPIs are more open to manipulation than profit; much will depend on the independence/objectivity of the data gathering process – but clearly IF NFPIs were easier to manipulate then this would not be considered as an advantage anyway.

26   The correct answer is: Internal business processes.

27   The correct answer is: Invest in project B.

	Current position	Project A	Project B
Investment	$18m	$2m	$3m
Forecast annual operating profit	$3m	$0.26m	$0.54m
ROCE (profit / investment)	16.7%	13%	18%

Project A does meet the criteria set by Division W's Head Office but if adopted it would dilute the existing ROCE of 16.7% and therefore would worsen Division W's reported performance. Based on this Division W would not accept project A. Project B will improve Division W's reported performance and therefore will be accepted.

28   The correct answer is:

Difficult to use to compare divisions.	RI
Likely to lead to sub-optimal decision-making.	ROI
May lead to information overload.	Balanced scorecard
Hard to use because of the complications in calculations.	EVA

Note that EVA is an absolute measure like RI and is therefore also hard to use to compare divisions – but this is not the main problem with EVA and each statement can only be matched to a single technique.

29   The correct answers are:

- Video conferencing has consistently grown in popularity
- The number of miles travelled by employees has fallen

	20X1	20X2	20X3
Miles travelled per employee	50	50	50
CO_2 emissions per mile	0.075	0.08	0.08
CO_2 emissions per member of staff	0.375	0.4	0.4

Note on incorrect answers:

As shown above the fall in CO_2 emissions appears to be due to the fall in the number of staff, not because of less travel or lower CO_2 emissions per mile travelled. So video conferencing, although popular, does not appear to be reducing M&M's environmental impact.

30   The correct answer is: Asset turnover 1.125   Operating margin 22.2%.

Operating margin is operating profit / sales.

Asset turnover = sales / (non-current assets + net current assets).

31   The correct answer is: Benchmarking against a company outside the parcel delivery sector with a reputation for excellent logistics.

Given D Co's need for a strategic breakthrough then new thinking will be required – and this is most likely to be available from partnering with, and analyzing, a high performing company outside D Co's industry.

Notes on incorrect answers:

- Competitive benchmarking

    - While useful it is not going to be **enough** for D Co to copy existing practice.

- Joining an industry database to analyse performance against KPIs for the parcel delivery industry – this will not identify best practice in the parcel delivery industry but only average performance; again this will not be enough for D Co.

- Internal benchmarking – D Co is underperforming so is unlikely to not allow D Co to identify dramatic performance improvements.

---

32   The correct answer is: Care must be taken to ensure that the innovation and learning measures complement the key internal business and customer measures.

It is essential that the measures in the balanced scorecard are consistent with each other and these observations seem fair and valid.

Notes on incorrect answers:

Two of the statements are not unreasonable (maximum of two measures, weighting of the measures) but cannot be said to be 'true': more than two measures may sometimes be appropriate.

Having more than two measures for each part of the scorecard MAY be appropriate but also may create information overload, so again this cannot be said to be 'true'.

---

33   The correct answer is: Neither ROI or RI would incorrectly reject project 315.

The project's return is 1.75 / 25 = 7%.

This is below the minimum threshold of 8% and therefore it should be rejected.

The project would be rejected using RI because it delivers negative residual income (1.75 – 0.08 × 25 = -0.25m).

The project would be accepted using ROI because the project's return is above the company's current ROI of 5%.

Therefore neither technique (for different reasons) incorrectly rejects the project – RI correctly rejects the project and ROI incorrectly accepts it.

---

34   The correct answer is: $18.

The true cost of the internal transfer is the relevant cost of internal sales ie lost sales revenue less saved external packaging costs. This is $20 – $2 = $18.

Alternatively to work out the lost contribution we can multiply the market price by 0.3 (reflecting the 30% contribution / sales margin). This gives 20 × 0.3 = $6 / kg of opportunity cost.

Variable cost = 0.7 × $20 = $14 but this includes packaging costs which would not be incurred internally so this cost is adjusted to $14 – $2 = $12.

The cost of the transfer can then be assessed as variable cost + opportunity cost = $12 + $6 = $18.

---

35 The correct answers are:

- A two-part tariff system could be introduced.
- A full cost + basis could be used as the transfer price.

Both of these will be simple ways of ensuring that Division Z takes a share of the gain from the transfer. A two part tariff simply involves a lumps sum payment in addition to the payment of a transfer price based on a variable cost.

Notes on incorrect answers:

- A dual tariff transfer pricing system could be introduced.

  - This involves Division Z billing Division T at a high price and Division Z recording the cost in its books at variable cost – and Head office maintaining an account showing the difference between these amounts. However this is complex and against the spirit of the statement made by Head Office.

- An opportunity cost basis could be used.

  - This IS the basis of the CURRENT price, there is not opportunity cost because Division Z has surplus capacity.

---

36 The correct answer is: The current transfer price recognizes the true cost of the internally transferred units and therefore should not be changed.

The true cost of the internal transfer is the relevant cost of internal sales ie the variable cost of producing a unit (there is no opportunity cost because the division has surplus capacity).

Variable cost = $10 – $3 contribution = $7 but this includes selling costs which would not be incurred internally so this cost is adjusted to $7 – $2 = $5.

The transfer price has therefore been set at a level that will cover the relevant cost of an internal transfer. So internal transfers will still happen.

If more effort is made to sell externally then this will not be at the expense of internal sales because there is spare capacity at Division X.

---

37 The correct answers are:

- Redundancy costs for European workers that are affected by this investment.
- Opportunity cost of lost sales due to disruption to production caused by the investment.

Notes on incorrect answers:

- Sales revenue from the products being sold by the Asian factory.

  - This would occur anyway even if the products were made in Europe (the motive for the investment is to reduce costs).

- A cut in dividends that would be needed to free up cash for the project.
- Interest costs on a loan that would be taken out to build the Asian factory.

  - Both the interest and dividends are financing costs and would be accounted for by using the cost of capital to discount the project's operating cash flows.

38 The correct answer is: $207,550.

Time	0	3	4	
Expected value of saving	100,000	75,000	75,000	
df	1	0.751	0.683	1,000
Present value	100,000	56,325	51,225	$207,550

The expected value of the savings in year 3 and 4 represent the lease saved of $300,000 multiplied by the probability of this saving (25%). Note that the refurbishment costs for Site A are definitely saved.

If you have chosen 107,550 you have forgotten the saving at time 0.

If you have chosen the higher numbers then you have forgotten that the lease payments are not definitely saved.

---

39 The correct answers are:

- The impact on Spice Co's brand name of exiting from this market.
- The future prospects for NT sales.

Comment on incorrect answers:

- The overspend on NT's set-up costs.

  – Though serious, this is a sunk cost and not relevant for decision making.

- The losses being made by NT.

  – NT is making a positive contribution so the fact that it is loss making is not relevant because profits are influenced by fixed overheads which may not be saved if production ceases.

- The price that the NT is being sold for.

  – This influences contribution, this is the factor that need to be considered. Future price levels are a significant issue but not the current price.

---

40 The correct answer is: $39,648.

Tax cash flows

Time	0	1	2
Written value of the investment	1,200,000	960,000	768,000
Claim (25% of b/f value)	240,000	192,000	153,600
Tax saved (25% of claim, 1 year delay)	60,000	48,000	
df at 10%	1	0.909	0.826
PV		54,540	39,648

Note that the question asks for the present value of the cash flows ARISING in time 2 not the cash flows from the tax depreciation arising in time 2.

---

41 The correct answers are:

- Managers understand IRR better than NPV.
- There is uncertainty over the appropriate cost of capital to use.

IRR is a percentage measure and so is easier for non-financial managers to understand, it does not require a precise cost of capital (although IRR needs to be compared to the expected return in order to make an investment decision).

Note that IRR (unlike ARR) does allow for the time value of money.

IRR is a % measure, if an absolute measure is required then NPV would be chosen.

---

42   The correct answer is: $74,086.

Time	1-4
Cash flow	74,086
Discount factor 12%	3.037
Required PV	225,000

Cash flow is calculated as 225,000 / 3.037

---

43   The correct answer is: Type A will be chosen, assuming the financial analysis has been performed correctly.

NPV should guide the investment decision, unless there is capital rationing with divisible projects in which case the profitability index should be used.

Notes on incorrect answers:

- In the absence of capital rationing constraints, both type A and type B should be fully financed.
    - Type A and type B are alternatives to each other so this is not true.
- At a cost of capital of higher than 22%, type B will be chosen.
    - Not true if the cost of capital is above 30%.
- IRR is not appropriate for this decision because it ignores the time value of money.
    - No, this is true of ARR but not IRR.

---

44   The correct answer is: It will be more accurate to discount the money cash flows using the 10% cost of capital.

We can assume that the 10% return includes an expectation of inflation, so it is a money cost of capital.

It is more accurate to use this approach because although all the operating cash flows are inflating at the SAME rate (which normally means you can use the real cost of capital) actually in the case the tax saved from capital allowances will not inflate. This means that inflation does have an impact ie it reduces the value of the tax savings from capital allowances. And this means that it is more accurate to adopt this approach.

---

45   The correct answer is: 2.8.

Depreciation is 100,000 / 4 operating years = 25,000 per year.

Cash flows are therefore estimated to be 25 (000s) higher than the cash flows given in the question.

Time	0	1	2	3	4	5
Cash flow ($'000s)	-100		45	65	70	85
Cumulative cash flow ($'000s)			-55	10		
Payback after 2 years			-55			
Cash flow during year 3			65			
Payback (2 + 55 / 65)			2.8 years			

46 The correct answers are:

- Payback should be emphasised much more strongly given VFD's circumstances.

- VFD should change its simple payback period target of 2 years to a discounted (adjusted) payback period of 2 years.

Payback does emphasise short-term liquidity and it is important for all companies, but small companies especially, to manage their cash flow carefully. Discounted pay back periods take into account the time value of money – because a project will take longer to pay-back in discounted terms then changing to a discounted payback period will place even stronger emphasis on liquidity issues (which seems appropriate for VFD Co).

Notes on incorrect answers:

- Project investment should be suspended during periods of cash shortages.

  - This may be needed in a crisis but as a general statement it is not true and will almost certainly damage the value of a company. We are told that VFD Co is experiencing cash flow pressures but not that it is in a crisis.

- VFD needs to focus on short-term profitability so it should primarily use ARR as its main project appraisal technique.

  - Unlikely to be true, the focus should be on short-term cash flow, not short-term profit.

---

47 The correct answer is: 14.6%.

Time	1	2
	750,000	750,000
Compound at 10%	1.1	1
Terminal value	825,000	750,000
Total terminal value	1,575,000	
Investment	1,200,000	
Return over 2 years	(1,575 / 1,200)	= 1.3125
Return pa	= 1.3125	= 1.146 ie 14.6%

Notes on incorrect answers:

18.3% is the standard IRR (calculated using the formula).

19.8% is also possible to calculate using the IRR formula if you have input the data incorrectly.

16.5% is obtained if you have incorrectly compounded the cash flows at 17%.

---

48 The correct answer is: $148,109.

The present value of the buying option is as follows:

Time	0	5
Outlay	-1,000,000	
Disposal proceeds		600,000
df 8%	1	0.681
PV	-1,000,000	408,600
Total NPV	-591,400	

To match this the annual rental payments would need to have a present value pf $591,400.

This is the equivalent of an annual cost of $148,109 as shown below:

Time	1 to 5
Rent	-148,109
df 8%	3.993
PV	-591,400
The rent is calculated as	-591,400 / 3.993

49   The correct answers are:

- The MIRR will be lower than the IRR.
- The MIRR will be above the cost of capital.

MIRR will be consistent with NPV, so if there is a positive NPV at 10% then the MIRR will be above 10%. However, one of the features of IRR is that it assumes that cash inflows from the project are re-invested at the IRR (here 20%) whereas MIRR assumes that the returns are reinvested to earn a 10% return (ie the cost of capital). As a result MIRR will be below IRR here.

---

50   The correct answer is: 99.

The fact that the projects are indivisible means that the profitability index (PI) is not relevant (Using the profitability index generates the solution of 114).

We need to identify the affordable combinations of projects, these are:

Combination of projects	Total cost ($'000s)	Total NPV ($'000s)
1,3,4	200	96
2,3	190	99
2,4	140	83

Note that it is not correct to add the cash that is not spent (eg there is 60k unspent if projects 2 and 3 are funded) to the NPV (this is where the other incorrect answers come from) because the NPV is measuring the extra value that is created and the unspent money is not extra value.

---

51   The correct answers are:

- Rank the projects using MIRR.
- Rank the projects using the profitability index.

MIRR shows the return on any funds invested, where MIRR is high the profitability index will also be high. So either method can be used to rank competing projects.

Notes on incorrect answers:

- Rank the projects using NPV.

    - This would be appropriate only if projects are not divisible.

- Use external sources of finance eg borrowing.

    - Soft capital rationing is where management have decided not to raise finance (possibly due to concerns over gearing) so this would not be a practical suggestion.

---

52   The correct answer is: $18,503 for a 1 year replacement cycle.

The equivalent annual cost for the 1 year cycle is the NPV of $16,819 / discount factor for 1 year (0.909) = $18,503.

For 2 years the calculations are:

Time	0	1	2
Purchase	($25,000)		
Running cost		($2,000)	
Net cash flows	($25,000)	($2,000)	($6,500)
Discount @ 10%	1	0.909	0.826
Present value	-25,000	-1,818	-5,369
Total present value		-32,187	
Cumulative discount factor for 1 year		1.736	
Equivalent annual cost		-18,541	

This is worse than year 1 and given the nature of this business there would be no point in using older cars if it does not save money (we are told that customers value having newer vehicles) so the Year 1 cycle is best.

If you calculated $12,743 you forgot that there is no disposal value in time 1.

The negative NPV arises because the revenue from leasing the cars has not been included in the analysis. The analysis focuses only on costs.

---

53 The correct answers are:

- An increase in the volatility of the oil price
- A longer licence period
- Tighter regulations over the award of licences to drill
- A rise in the demand for natural gas

An increase in the volatility of the oil price will make it likely that there will be a period of high oil prices that will justify the investment in the oil field. Oil can be stored and sold when the price is high.

A longer licence period makes it more probable that changes in costs or oil prices will occur – which raises the potential value of this option.

Tighter regulations will restrict the supply of oil and this will help to drive up its price.

A rise in demand for natural gas will enhance the value of this oil field because it also contains significant reserves of natural gas.

---

54 The correct answer is: $300.

Payoff table

Order size	20	40	60
Demand			
20	300	100	-100
40	300	600	400
60	300	600	900

A full payoff table is not required here but is shown to aid your understanding.

The worst outcome for each order size is as follows:

Order size	20	40	60
Worst outcome	300	100	-100

The best of these worst outcomes is associated with the lowest order size.

The probabilities provided here are not relevant to this analysis.

---

55 The correct answer is:

Based on subjective probabilities.	Expected values
Ignores the importance of later cash flows.	Discounted payback period
Only considers the impact of changing one variable at a time.	Sensitivity analysis
Complex and time-consuming.	Simulation

Expected values are based on probabilities that are often highly subjective.

Discounted payback period fails to take into account the cash flows that occur after the payback period.

Sensitivity analysis examines the change in a specific variable (and only that variable) that is required for the project NPV to fall to zero.

Simulations are based on a number of possible business scenarios which have to be identified and modelled. This is time consuming.

56 The correct answer is: 1.9%.

Time	0	1 to 4	discount factor (10%)	Heading
Contribution (420k – 160k)		260,000	3.17	824,200
Fixed costs		-50,000	3.17	-158,500
Investment	-650,000			-650,000
Total				15,700
Sensitivity	= Project NPV		= 15,700	= 1.9
	PV of contribution = 824,200			

---

57 The correct answer is: Field W.

Regret vs best outcome: summary.

Scenario	Best outcome	W field	X field	Y field	Z field
1	X = $100m	$10m (100 – 90)	0	$80m (100 – 20)	$40m (100 – 60)
2	X = $80m	$10m (80 – 70)	0	$40m (80 – 40)	$30m (80 – 50)
3	Y = $90m	$25m (90 – 65)	$30m (90 – 60)	0	$50m (90 – 40)
Maximum regret		$25m	$30m	$80m	$50m

The option with the lowest maximum regret is the W field.

---

58 The correct answer is: 40.6.

The expected value of the project if it proceeds is (120 × 0.5) + (80 × 0.5) = $100m then deducting $40m for the land = $60m.

Therefore the value of the land if planning permission is refused is $3m

The overall expected profit is therefore:

($120m × 0.4) + ($80m × 0.4) + ($3m × 0.2) – $40m = $40.6m.

---

59 The correct answers are:

- Business continuity insurance
- Diversify by building another smaller warehouse in another part of Europe

These are classic responses to managing risks that are unlikely but would be serious if they did occur (using the TARA framework).

Taking no action would be exposing shareholders to excessively high levels of risk.

Controlling the performance of the warehouse would be more appropriate if this was a LIKELY risk, and there is no indication that this is the case here.

---

60 The correct answer is: 300,000.

Order size	
50,000	= (0.1 × 100) + (0.4 × 100) + (0.3 × 100) + (0.2 × 100) = 100
300,000	= (0.1 × -1,150) + (0.4 × 1,100) + (0.3 × 1,100) + (0.2 × 1,100) = 875
1,000,000	= (0.1 × -4,650) + (0.4 × -2,400) + (0.3 × 3,900) + (0.2 × 3,900) = 525
10,000,000	= (0.1 × -49,650) + (0.4 × -47,400) + (0.3 × -41,100) + (0.2 × 39,900) = -28,275

Mathematical tables

PRESENT VALUE TABLE

Present value of 1.00 unit of currency, that is $(1+r)^{-n}$ where r = interest rate; n = number of periods until payment of receipt.

Periods (n)	Interest rates (r)									
	1%	2%	3%	4%	5%	6%	7%	8%	9%	10%
1	0.990	0.980	0.971	0.962	0.952	0.943	0.935	0.926	0.917	0.909
2	0.980	0.961	0.943	0.925	0.907	0.890	0.873	0.857	0.842	0.826
3	0.971	0.942	0.915	0.889	0.864	0.840	0.816	0.794	0.772	0.751
4	0.961	0.924	0.888	0.855	0.823	0.792	0.763	0.735	0.708	0.683
5	0.951	0.906	0.863	0.822	0.784	0.747	0.713	0.681	0.650	0.621
6	0.942	0.888	0.837	0.790	0.746	0.705	0.666	0.630	0.596	0.564
7	0.933	0.871	0.813	0.760	0.711	0.665	0.623	0.583	0.547	0.513
8	0.923	0.853	0.789	0.731	0.677	0.627	0.582	0.540	0.502	0.467
9	0.914	0.837	0.766	0.703	0.645	0.592	0.544	0.500	0.460	0.424
10	0.905	0.820	0.744	0.676	0.614	0.558	0.508	0.463	0.422	0.386
11	0.896	0.804	0.722	0.650	0.585	0.527	0.475	0 429	0.388	0.350
12	0.887	0.788	0.701	0.625	0.557	0.497	0.444	0.397	0.356	0.319
13	0.879	0.773	0.681	0.601	0.530	0.469	0.415	0.368	0.326	0.290
14	0.870	0.758	0.681	0.577	0.505	0.442	0.388	0.340	0.299	0.263
15	0.861	0.743	0.642	0.555	0.481	0.417	0.362	0.315	0.275	0.239
16	0.853	0.728	0.623	0.534	0.458	0.394	0.339	0.292	0.252	0.218
17	0.844	0.714	0.605	0.513	0.436	0.371	0.317	0.270	0.231	0.198
18	0.836	0.700	0.587	0.494	0.416	0.350	0.296	0.250	0.212	0.180
19	0.828	0.686	0.570	0.475	0.396	0.331	0.277	0.232	0.194	0.164
20	0.820	0.673	0.554	0.456	0.377	0.312	0.258	0.215	0.178	0.149

Periods (n)	Interest rates (r)									
	11%	12%	13%	14%	15%	16%	17%	18%	19%	20%
1	0.901	0.893	0.885	0.877	0.870	0.862	0.855	0.847	0.840	0.833
2	0.812	0.797	0.783	0.769	0.756	0.743	0.731	0.718	0.706	0.694
3	0.731	0.712	0.693	0.675	0.658	0.641	0.624	0.609	0.593	0.579
4	0.659	0.636	0.613	0.592	0.572	0.552	0.534	0.516	0.499	0.482
5	0.593	0.567	0.543	0.519	0.497	0.476	0.456	0.437	0.419	0.402
6	0.535	0.507	0.480	0.456	0.432	0.410	0.390	0.370	0.352	0.335
7	0.482	0.452	0.425	0.400	0.376	0.354	0.333	0.314	0.296	0.279
8	0.434	0.404	0.376	0.351	0.327	0.305	0.285	0.266	0.249	0.233
9	0.391	0.361	0.333	0.308	0.284	0.263	0.243	0.225	0.209	0.194
10	0.352	0.322	0.295	0.270	0.247	0.227	0.208	0.191	0.176	0.162
11	0.317	0.287	0.261	0.237	0.215	0.195	0.178	0.162	0.148	0.135
12	0.286	0.257	0.231	0.208	0.187	0.168	0.152	0.137	0.124	0.112
13	0.258	0.229	0.204	0.182	0.163	0.145	0.130	0.116	0.104	0.093
14	0.232	0.205	0.181	0.160	0.141	0.125	0.111	0.099	0.088	0.078
15	0.209	0.183	0.160	0.140	0.123	0.108	0.095	0.084	0.079	0.065
16	0.188	0.163	0.141	0.123	0.107	0.093	0.081	0.071	0.062	0.054
17	0.170	0.146	0.125	0.108	0.093	0.080	0.069	0.060	0.052	0.045
18	0.153	0.130	0.111	0.095	0.081	0.069	0.059	0.051	0.044	0.038
19	0.138	0.116	0.098	0.083	0.070	0.060	0.051	0.043	0.037	0.031
20	0.124	0.104	0.087	0.073	0.061	0.051	0.043	0.037	0.031	0.026

Cumulative present value of 1.00 unit of currency per annum, Receivable or Payable at the end of each year for n years $\dfrac{1-(1+r)^{-n}}{r}$

Periods (n)	Interest rates (r)									
	1%	2%	3%	4%	5%	6%	7%	8%	9%	10%
1	0.990	0.980	0.971	0.962	0.952	0.943	0.935	0.926	0.917	0.909
2	1.970	1.942	1.913	1.888	1.859	1.833	1.808	1.783	1.759	1.736
3	2.941	2.884	2.829	2.775	2.723	2.673	2.624	2.577	2.531	2.487
4	3.902	3.808	3.717	3.630	3.546	3.465	3.387	3.312	3.240	3.170
5	4.853	4.713	4.580	4.452	4.329	4.212	4.100	3.993	3.890	3.791
6	5.795	5.601	5.417	5.242	5.076	4.917	4.767	4.623	4.486	4.355
7	6.728	6.472	6.230	6.002	5.786	5.582	5.389	5.206	5.033	4.868
8	7.652	7.325	7.020	6.733	6.463	6.210	5.971	5.747	5.535	5.335
9	8.566	8.162	7.786	7.435	7.108	6.802	6.515	6.247	5.995	5.759
10	9.471	8.983	8.530	8.111	7.722	7.360	7.024	6.710	6.418	6.145
11	10.368	9.787	9.253	8.760	8.306	7.887	7.499	7.139	6.805	6.495
12	11.255	10.575	9.954	9.385	8.863	8.384	7.943	7.536	7.161	6.814
13	12.134	11.348	10.635	9.986	9.394	8.853	8.358	7.904	7.487	7.103
14	13.004	12.106	11.296	10.563	9.899	9.295	8.745	8.244	7.786	7.367
15	13.865	12.849	11.938	11.118	10.380	9.712	9.108	8.559	8.061	7.606
16	14.718	13.578	12.561	11.652	10.838	10.106	9.447	8.851	8.313	7.824
17	15.562	14.292	13.166	12.166	11.274	10.477	9.763	9.122	8.544	8.022
18	16.398	14.992	13.754	12.659	11.690	10.828	10.059	9.372	8.756	6.201
19	17.226	15.679	14.324	13.134	12.085	11.158	10.336	9.604	8.950	8.365
20	18.046	16.351	14.878	13.590	12.462	11.470	10.594	9.818	9.129	8.514

Periods (n)	Interest rates (r)									
	11%	12%	13%	14%	15%	16%	17%	18%	19%	20%
1	0.901	0.893	0.885	0.877	0.870	0.862	0.855	0.847	0.840	0.833
2	1.713	1.690	1.668	1.647	1.626	1.605	1.585	1.566	1.547	1.528
3	2.444	2.402	2.361	2.322	2.283	2.246	2.210	2.174	2.140	2.106
4	3.102	3.037	2.974	2.914	2.855	2.798	2.743	2.690	2.639	2.589
5	3.696	3.605	3.517	3.433	3.352	3.274	3.199	3.127	3.058	2.991
6	4.231	4.111	3.998	3.889	3.784	3.685	3.589	3.498	3.410	3.326
7	4.712	4.564	4.423	4.288	4.180	4.039	3.922	3.812	3.706	3.605
8	5.146	4.968	4.799	4.639	4.487	4.344	4.207	4.078	3.954	3.837
9	5.537	5.328	5.132	4.946	4.772	4.607	4.451	4.303	4.163	4.031
10	5.889	5.650	5.426	5.216	5.019	4.833	4 659	4.494	4.339	4.192
11	6.207	5.938	5.687	5.453	5.234	5.029	4.836	4.656	4.486	4.327
12	6.492	6.194	5.918	5.860	5.421	5.197	4.988	4.793	4.611	4.439
13	6.750	6.424	6.122	5.842	5.583	5.342	5.118	4.910	4.715	4.533
14	6.982	6.628	6.302	6.002	5.724	5.468	5.229	5.008	4.802	4.611
15	7.191	6.811	6.462	6.142	5.847	5.575	5.324	5.092	4.876	4.675
16	7.379	6.974	6.604	6.265	5.954	5.668	5.405	5.162	4.938	4.730
17	7.549	7.120	6.729	6.373	6.047	5.749	5.475	5.222	4.990	4.775
18	7.702	7.250	6.840	6.467	6.128	5.818	5.534	5.273	5.033	4.812
19	7.839	7.366	6.938	6.550	6.198	5.877	5.584	5.316	5.070	4.843
20	7.963	7.489	7.025	6.623	6.259	5.929	5.628	5.353	5.101	4.870